THE
POWER OF
PARADOX

ADVANCE PRAISE FOR THE BOOK

'*The Power of Paradox* skilfully guides readers to explore life's inherent contradictions with wisdom and courage. Daaji's insights empower us to find inner peace amidst life's dualities, offering a timeless path to clarity and resilience in our complex world'—**Ram Nath Kovind, former President of India**

'In *The Power of Paradox*, Daaji unravels the dualities that shape our lives, leading us to profound insights hidden within contradictions. With his gentle wisdom, he shows us how the dance between opposites can ignite transformation. This book is a powerful reminder that true growth often lies in the spaces we least expect'—**Shekhar Kapur, award-winning film-maker and storyteller**

'In *The Power of Paradox,* Daaji explores the surprising balance between seemingly opposing forces within us—logic and intuition, mind and heart, ambition and contentment. With clarity and compassion, he shows us a transformative path to embracing life's contradictions as gateways to deeper wisdom and inner peace'—**Kabir Bedi, veteran actor and speaker**

'The conflicts, paradoxes and uncertainties of daily living provide surprising trail heads into a richer understanding of our life. In a down-to-earth style, Daaji invites us to gently turn toward those with courage and curiosity in order to deepen our hearts'—**Tobin Hart, professor, University of West Georgia, and author of *The Integrative Mind: Transformative Education for a World on Fire* and *The Secret Spiritual World of Children***

THE
POWER OF
PARADOX

Insights and Lessons
from Apparent
Contradictions

DAAJI

KAMLESH D. PATEL

PENGUIN
ANANDA

An imprint of Penguin Random House

PENGUIN ANANDA

Penguin Ananda is an imprint of the Penguin Random House group of companies
whose addresses can be found at global.penguinrandomhouse.com

Published by Penguin Random House India Pvt. Ltd
4th Floor, Capital Tower 1, MG Road,
Gurugram 122 002, Haryana, India

First published in Penguin Ananda by Penguin Random House India 2024

ISBN 9780143459309

Typeset in Adobe Caslon Pro by MAP Systems, Bengaluru, India
Printed at Thomson Press India Ltd, New Delhi

www.penguin.co.in

The words of truth are always paradoxical.
—Lao Tzu

Contents

Part 3: Life's Meaning and Purpose

Part 4: Wisdom and Philosophical Concepts

Part 5: Spirituality and Holistic Well-Being

Part 6: Toolbox: Suggested Practices and Exercises

Introduction

I studied at L.M. College of Pharmacy in Ahmedabad (1974–1980), where I had a group of almost twenty friends. We watched movies, played sports, enjoyed studies, shared dreams, and above all, we meditated together. The principal of our college, Dr Banhu Bahen Trivedi, was a woman of regal stature, with a compassionate heart. She liked our group. I still remember her gaze; whenever she saw us, she had this smile that was a mix of wonder and intrigue. Perhaps she was thinking, 'What are these boys up to?'

I was the faculty representative in my college. In 1980, there was a critical day in my life—an election for the dean of Pharmacy. Banhu Bahen, the principal, was contesting for this position. The other candidate was Professor Chauhan, also a well-respected teacher. Both had their camps supporting them. It so happened that the election ended in a tie. In those days, the rule book read that in case of a tie, the faculty representative cast the deciding vote. I had to choose between two wonderful individuals, both of whom were capable. They both liked me and guided me. And the next big step in their career came down to my vote. I was pressured directly and indirectly by friends, teachers and even some local business leaders who tried to sway my vote for one or the other.

I did not want to be in this situation. It was not fair to put the onus of such a decision on a student. What did I do to deserve this conundrum? No matter what I decided, I would still make someone whom I respected unhappy. Life isn't fair. The crucible of choices I was thrust into, pained me. In the face of all that pressure, my refuge was meditation. It helped me break free from the paradox of good versus right, I chose to dive into the wellspring of my inner strength. With this inner clarity, I followed my heart and cast my vote. Banhu Bahen was chosen as the new dean.

You may recall similar situations in your life where you were torn by the stress of making decisions where either both options seemed good, or neither did, or you could not choose between the good and the not optimal.

Enter the paradox—a confrontation with choices that can result in stress, dilemma and angst. Paradoxes and the situations they create are something we are all familiar with. Should I choose the job that pays me more or the job that values my loyalty? Should I enjoy life now or invest for the future? Should I be spontaneous or disciplined? Should I move back home and take care of my parents, or should I stay put for the welfare of my children? A paradox can scramble the mind. What follows is a loop of stress, tension, indecision and constant worry about whether we made the right choice.

As you will soon discover, a big source of our worries stems from the paradoxes we face in life and the uncertainty between two choices that we don't yet fully understand.

Paradoxes are like shadows at dusk—subtle, shifting and often unnoticed in the fading light. We may not always see them clearly, but they are there, shaping our perception of reality. It is only when we pause and look closely that we begin to understand their quiet yet profound influence on our lives. Even though the paradoxes can seem evasive, the symptoms they exhibit are pervasive: stress, dilemmas and confusion.

Nothing Stays the Same

Whether you find yourself balancing the demands of your inner and outer life, prioritizing between the short term and the long term, or pursuing an authentic relationship with yourself and others, at the heart of each inquiry lies an underlying paradox. It tests us with choices. While we crave clean choices that are black and white, a paradox offers a spectrum of foggy greys. How to make decisions in such a haze so we are at peace and free from regret? And how to accept the haze as the path to understanding? The answer lies in harnessing the power of paradox. We can harness it only when we understand a paradox and how it affects us. We must be prepared to explore the same paradox a day, month and years down the road.

'No man steps in the same river twice,' wrote Heraclitus, the sixth-century Greek philosopher.[1] How is that possible? Because it is not the same river and you are not the same person. Still confusing? Let me explain. Heraclitus believed that everything, everyone—the entire universe—is in a constant state of flux. A translation closer to the original captures the feeling of the flux even better:

'The river where you set your foot just now is gone—those waters giving way to this, now this.'[2] It is true—we change, our beliefs change, our purposes change, the meanings of words change and times change, the reason for examining the paradox might change too. So, continuing to increase our knowledge, self-reflection and problem-solving must be an ongoing process.

The Dynamics of a Paradox

A paradox arises from the logical tension between seemingly valid statements or ideas that cannot be true at the same time. 'The more you try to impress people, the less impressed they will be'; 'The more you learn, the more you realize how little you know'; in the words of one of my teachers, 'The more I know, the more I acknowledge I know nothing'; and 'The more you hate a trait in someone else, the more likely it is that you are avoiding it in yourself' are all examples of paradoxes.

What is not a paradox? Ambiguity and irony are not paradoxes. Neither are simple contradictions, coincidences, riddles or puzzles. Scientists try to solve the paradoxes of physics; comedians find the paradoxes of everyday life by highlighting hypocrisy, deconstructing institutions and subverting expectations. Yogis and spiritual leaders believe we can glimpse the spiritual world while walking in the physical, which is the greatest paradox of all.

Understanding paradoxical statements requires us to put a pause on logic, push the boundaries of our thinking, question the established beliefs and explore the complexities of the world around us. This way, we can derive a higher meaning from the statements about day-to-day life on earth, such as 'less is more' and 'you have to spend money to make money'. Embracing paradoxes as opportunities for growth allows us to navigate the complexities of life with greater wisdom and insight. By challenging our assumptions of the nature of logic, reasoning and reality, a paradox stimulates critical thinking, expands our mental horizons, enhances our problem-solving abilities, and encourages philosophical inquiry and spiritual transformation.

Recognizing the complex interplay between paradoxical elements underscores the fundamental interconnectedness of all things. It's like the threads of a vast web, where every tension or movement on one strand affects the entire structure, reminding us that nothing exists in isolation.

The dynamic tension between opposites gives birth to and sustains the constantly changing and ever-evolving elements of the universe. The swirling black-and-white circle of the t'ai chi symbol shows the interaction of opposites, illustrating the universal principle that if one half of a pair (let us call this half A) does not exist, the other half (B) does not exist either. Without A, we have no B. The whole does not exist. Nothing exists. We have no highway, no back road, no guard rails to keep us on track and no direction to head to. We have nothing to move from and nothing to move towards.

We need both sides of the paradox to make a whole. We must have both light and dark, inside and outside, stop and go, minute details and the overall perspective, tight focus and a wide lens. Without the interplay between these pairs, there is only stagnation and decay. There is no life. Creative tension is essential for life and growth. We also need space in between the two halves. This is the space created by examining their interplay. We open this space through inquiry, observation and reflection; by finding the differences and similarities and the truth and falsity of the two halves. Whether we are trying to solve or observe, this space is also where possibility exists.

When we come across paradoxes, the inherent contradictions need not hold us back. Instead, we can use them to help us fine-tune our understanding of reality. In this book, we will explore what lies beneath the mainstream beliefs that we come across every day. By uncovering what lies underneath, we can reorient our life and gain a profound understanding of the world. A clear orientation allows us to interact with our fellow beings, discussing mundane topics or more serious spiritual matters—be it with family, at work, place of worship or a social get-together. With this orientation, we can make the most of our efforts, engagements and endeavours on the journey towards a grand finale of existence with truth, bliss and beyond. That is why a fresh perspective and clarity are needed to solve the inconsistencies in these statements and guide our minds positively. We need clarity and courage, discernment and focus, *viveka* and *vairagya* in Sanskrit, to be purposeful in our lives. Viveka and vairagya are the two fundamental qualities of the heart that, when cultivated with the help of the Heartfulness way of living, provide the bedrock for a good life.

Approaching Paradoxes

In this book, I explore twenty-seven paradoxes that we come across in our lives from the fresh perspective of combined spiritual and scientific inquiry. I share insights to help understand these paradoxes and work with them. It is vital to learn this skill because paradoxes are portals for growth, provided you know how to identify, embrace and transcend the paradox. When you do that, you become a new you. A paradox is a launch pad to get to the next level of growth. You grow from worry to wisdom, from stress to strength, from bondage to freedom and from tension to tenacity.

My personal experience tells me that when I explore a paradox, I open myself to experience the finer truths in life, which in turn brings clarity and confidence and invariably adds joy to my heart. I think everyone can experience this transition. Understanding these paradoxes in the right context and approaching them using a method that is right for you, helps provide you with the necessary clarity and perspective to keep discovering, exploring, contemplating and growing.

There are many ways to approach a paradox: looking at how both statements are true and how they aren't, digging deeper into the tangents that might emerge and assessing whether they are true or false. But while this book is definitely a discussion of paradoxes, it is not a philosophical or scientific text about how to solve them. Instead, I offer a simplified model that combines both logic and intuition based on personal experience. The following is a holistic framework for thinking about how individuals and philosophical traditions might approach paradoxes. I call it the DARE to RESOLVE framework. DARE is an acronym for the four approaches outlined in this framework. Dare also stands for the courage required to resolve paradoxes, which requires putting yourself, your beliefs and your behaviour based on those beliefs under the microscope. Daring to resolve takes bravery. You're going to turn your world inside out, shift your perspective, and look at yourself and your world in a whole new way.

Dismiss: This response involves rejecting the paradox as either based on a misunderstanding, misuse of language or not being a genuine problem. Those who dismiss a paradox might argue that the paradox arises from incorrect premises or a flawed reasoning process, thereby negating its significance.

Accept: Accepting a paradox involves acknowledging the paradox as an unresolved or potentially unresolvable issue within the current framework of understanding. This does not necessarily mean seeing the paradox as true in the conventional sense but recognizing its persistence in thought or theory without insisting on resolution. An example would be accepting the status quo because 'it's always been that way' or 'that's how we've always done it' or adhering to a rule while 'I don't make the rules; I just work here'.

Resolve: Resolution seeks to dissolve the paradox by addressing its underlying causes. This might involve refining definitions, adjusting the framework of understanding or showing how the apparent incongruency is only superficial and can be reconciled through deeper analysis.

Explore: Exploration views the paradox as fundamentally insightful or revealing about the nature of reality, language or thought. The paradox becomes a tool to explore implications, prompt further inquiry and expand the boundaries of understanding. It functions as a pointer to deeper truths or complexities that escape conventional logic.

While some traditions or thinkers might prioritize resolution (as seen in much of Western philosophy), others might find value in embracing the paradoxical (a more characteristic approach of certain Eastern philosophies). Where the mind and the heart meet, we gain a holistic understanding of these paradoxes with all their significance. I recommend a holistic approach to resolving and understanding the everyday paradoxes.

Paradoxes play a vital role in ancient wisdom texts. Paradoxes in these texts are not intended to give definitive answers but to encourage an ongoing process of reflection, self-discovery and the cultivation of wisdom. They emphasize the importance of direct experience, introspection and intuition as avenues for uncovering deeper truths.

Paradoxes in the *Tao Te Ching* challenge conventional thinking and offer insights into the nature of reality: 'The highest virtue is not virtuous. Therefore, it has virtue.'[3] In the Bhagavad Gita, Krishna reveals 'the sublime mystery' to Arjuna, explaining that 'while His essence permeates all existence, existence is empty of Him'.[4]

When great spiritual personalities such as Jesus, Mohammed, Lord Krishna, Ashtavakra and my spiritual teacher, Babuji, talk in a paradoxical manner, it is to keep us on our toes so we can think and come to our own heartfelt conclusions, and then implement those conclusions in our lives, based on our heart's clarity.

I suggest reading these chapters in order first, because a concept presented in one chapter might be explored deeply in a later chapter. After the first read, you can keep this book close at hand and read the chapter you feel drawn to or need at the time. Reminiscent of books such as *The Prophet* by Kahlil Gibran, this book too can serve as a reference, a resource to gain clarity about concepts or find answers to your questions.

* * *

Our life's journey is exceptionally challenging, no matter where we work or live or how much money we have. Cities are growing and rural areas diminishing. Our beliefs and emotions are sharply divided into distinct groups leaving no room for compromise. Social media, climate change, culture wars and wars between nations are putting an enormous stress on people. So, we must counter these negative forces with mental clarity and peaceful hearts.

From a very young age, I have been inspired to find answers by turning inwards, using the techniques of introspection and heart-based contemplation. In a short time, this approach changed my trajectory in life. It taught me to look at things in a more realistic and purposeful manner. This approach improves our discernment, which I consider essential for making good choices. Good choices are the ones that are right and making the right choices shapes our destiny.

My fervent hope is that these paradoxes become clearer, spark insights and offer valuable guidance to your life. Heartfulness is a set of practices that synthesizes the wonders of spirituality with the power of the rational mind. The combined power of heart and mind is unimaginable and takes us closer to experiencing the truths in our lives rather than just understanding them intellectually. This clarity enables the self-confidence and courage we need to lead a purposeful life.

The methods of Heartfulness practices sprinkled throughout this book will help you clear the cobwebs of the mind and unburden the heavy emotions of the heart. I hope you enjoy reading this book as much as I enjoyed writing it. I am certain that you will gain clarity and confidence reading it, and the book will help you in your personal life as well as your spiritual journey, allowing you to gain more clarity and aid and engineer more positive outcomes in your lives and relationships in our rapidly changing world.

Part 1

Personal Growth and Development

Stability Promotes Change

> One thing is for sure. If we are afraid of change, we will continue to accept the status quo, however terrible it may be.

In the first century BCE, King Herod the Great constructed Masada, a sprawling palace on a rocky plateau in the Judean Desert overlooking the Dead Sea, 20 km east of present-day Arad. Less than one hundred years later, the palace lay in ruins. In the next few centuries, wars destroyed the date palm crops of the desert. Its fruit was highly renowned for its healing properties. In the 1960s, hundreds of seeds from those dates were unearthed in what was left of the palace and in nearby caves. After being delicately nurtured in a warm water-hormone solution, seven seeds sprouted and rekindled fresh life into the date palms.

Despite two thousand years of brutal heat and wind, the life force within those seeds persisted. Serendipity preserved those seeds. Nature provided the care and nurturing that they needed for their transformation from seed to plant. We, too, possess a wellspring of wisdom within us—a reservoir of coded knowledge, the potential and the imperishable life in the seed. As individuals, we encounter periods of immense change, both personally and collectively. From career transitions to coping with loss and global upheavals, the ebb and flow of existence challenge our equilibrium. However, we are more resilient than we think we are. The wisdom rooted deep within our consciousness can enable us to remain steady during these times of rapid change.

I am sure you can relate to how unsettling it can feel when life changes dramatically from one day to the next. Maybe you have moved or gone on a trip and awakened in the night with no idea where you are. Or you have started a new job, and though it's a job you wanted, you feel a bit lost in your new environment. Perhaps even a bit estranged from yourself. You second guess the decision. These feelings pass, of course, but they can be uncomfortable. And these are the changes you *desired* and planned for.

So, it is not surprising that instead of flowing with change, we often seek stability during times of transition and seek change when our lives are stable. We have a complex relationship with change.

Drive reduction theory proposes that our body's needs drive actions to fulfil them. For example, when we feel thirsty, we are driven to find and drink water to reduce the thirst. This theory applies to our psychological states as well. When we feel we'd be better off in another job, we seek a new one. This drive may arise because we don't feel appreciated or challenged in our current job, or we could make more money elsewhere, or find greater opportunities for growth. Satisfying this drive for a new job requires us to accept a change in our situation and putting up with the discomfort that accompanies the change.

The change becomes too uncomfortable when the urgency to fulfil the need becomes too strong (we need that water or job *this minute*) or too weak (we cannot find the energy or will to find water or a job). We try to regain our equilibrium, or homeostasis, by dampening or raising our motivation for that change until the discomfort subsides.[1]

According to some psychologists, seeking stability is one of our primary human drives, along with the need for social acceptance and achievement. When we juxtapose this drive for stability with the need for greater achievement and acceptance, we realize that stability is obviously short-lived, and we ignite the ambition that creates change.[2] Whether the change is internal, i.e., for self-transformation, or external, we either want to change a situation we're unhappy with or we want to improve our current situation even though we aren't unhappy.

Self-Initiated Transformation

When you consider initiating external changes, weigh the benefits and discomforts against those of not making the change. You might ask yourself, 'Do I really want to transfer to another team at work, or do I want to avoid the upheaval, stay with my existing team where I need to meditate for five minutes every hour to tolerate my boss?'; 'Do I really want to leave this relationship in which I'm so miserable, or do I want to stay because I've invested so much time and effort?'

Let us now look at individual transformation, the change from within that is brought on by rigorous self-improvement practices such as introspection and meditation. In meditation practices such as mindfulness and heartfulness, we see growth and progress through experiencing different states of consciousness. This brings about different ideas, better understanding and new possibilities. Everything else—initiating change, planning for change, navigating change—flows from this point.

To begin this transformative journey, it is crucial to ask yourself whether you genuinely desire to undergo change or you would prefer to remain in the comfort zone within yourself, even though you're miserable. The question itself hints at the answer: you need to get out of your comfort zone. While the initial stages of change may look and feel unfamiliar, and you may experience discomfort, you gradually adapt to the new states of consciousness you experience. Once you realize these blissful states of newer levels of transformation, you will invite them.

Desired Versus Undesired Change

When we trigger change, we seek an unknown and uncertain future. At times, we begin by imagining the future situation as if it were familiar to us. For example, we might want to marry the partner of our dreams, and we envision moving to a new house in the suburbs, welcoming beautiful and healthy children and living happily ever after. Regardless of the circumstances, we initiate a change, believing it will improve our situation. We imagine, visualize and are convinced that we are going to be better off.

Of course, this type of change represents something we know we want. When there is a desire to change, it is easier to adjust and we are willing to expend the necessary energy—physically, emotionally and financially.

Change is more difficult and uncomfortable when it goes against what you might desire. When you are in love, you will happily adjust and willingly fulfil every little hint of your beloved's expectation without any resistance. But when you're not, even doing things you formerly liked to do will be a burden.

Managing Change

Although we can trigger change through our desire to improve the status quo, we must consider the obstacles and challenges that may arise in this process. One thing is certain: if we fear change or the uncertain outcome of that change, we'll continue accepting the status quo, even if we don't like it. Without proper planning and management, the process of change can create chaos and instability in our lives, despite our hopes for a smooth transition. For example, some people tolerate an abusive relationship for what they believe to be the sake of their children. In such a situation, taking the time to have some difficult and open conversations with the children is necessary. Such discussions can help gain the children's support, which is possible when they have a better understanding of the circumstances. This will make the decision to change more deliberate and allow people to avoid unnecessary and unplanned chaos. As a result, the transition will be easier for all involved.

Whatever the change, it demands that we make adjustments. The faster the change, the more rapid a process of adjustment is required. When a change is significant, the adjustment must be substantial and focused. It takes an enormous amount of personal and emotional energy to go through an adjustment process, so it's important to take care of ourselves during these times. This way, we can approach and navigate change with greater ease and resilience. I recommend taking a pause, breathing and making a positive affirmation to get through these times of rapid change.

At times, change demands expense. For example, relocating to a new house or city can be financially draining and destabilizing. At times, we may even run out of 'energy' before we finish the transition, which creates additional chaos. It's important to remember that setbacks and delays are common.

When we plan a change, it's mainly due to a desire to alter our personal status quo by setting goals and preparing to achieve them. The bigger the goal, the wider the gap between what is and what we intend to accomplish, and the greater the effort and input of energy needed. Change can be daunting and requires effort. Our brains may resist it due to its lazy nature. However, we can overcome this resistance by increasing our desire or passion for change and envisioning the positive outcomes that await us after it is accomplished.

Unlike planning for a change, when a change is thrust upon us, it tests our tenacity and character. What if change is unforeseen, such as a natural disaster or the sudden death of the breadwinner of the family? Such unplanned events can bring about catastrophic change and test the resilience of the strongest of us. Nothing will come to our aid other than our emotional strength and the community that stands with us during those times. For this reason, the investment we have made in developing the inner self and creating goodwill in the community will help us manage and endure as we go through unforeseen changes in our lives. The need for loving your neighbour, being part of an active community and maintaining a good relationship with your family members cannot be underestimated.

Managing the process of change is a skill we need to develop to reduce our arbitrary and inconsistent reactions to it. Developing an attitude of love, interest, passion and having fun can help us embrace and fully manifest any change that moves us towards our intended objective.

Aligning Transformation with Your Purpose

Now, it is worthwhile to ask yourself these questions: 'What is the greatest objective I want to set for myself, the one that will allow me to reconcile and integrate stability and change?' and 'Is all the chaos of change worth this great aspiration or adventure?' Because if the chaos is not worth it to you, you'll have a difficult time following through. In the epic Mahabharata, there is a story about Lord Krishna and Prince Arjuna during the Mahabharata war. Krishna wants to establish righteousness in the kingdom and inspires the confused, weak and reluctant Arjuna to steady himself, gather his courage and fight the cousins who have stolen part of his kingdom. Krishna's guidance is recounted in the important Hindu scripture, the Bhagavad Gita, where the war symbolizes the battle between our desires and the evil methods that we develop to attain them. Pursuing these methods eventually leads to discontentment, disharmony, anger, fear and confusion.

Krishna inspires Arjuna to perform his duty without attachment to the consequences, teaching him that a noble cause requires noble action. If we adopt such an understanding, we can attain stability in our minds and hearts, allowing us to fulfil our duty and responsibility to ourselves and the world around us, while bringing about positive and evolutionary change.

If a change is for the welfare of the self or the universe, it becomes evolutionary, bringing stability to our mental state even as our outer circumstances shift.

How You Might Approach This Paradox

In your lifetime, you'll have numerous opportunities to revisit this paradox. Certain times may call for different methods or a combination of them. You can also devise your own method to solve, explore or experience this paradox when it arises. Let us look at how you might apply one of the four fundamental responses outlined in the Introduction: dismiss, accept, resolve or explore (The DARE framework). Let's take a look at the options regarding seeking stability during change and change during stability.

> **Dismiss.** You might dismiss the premise altogether as either based on a misunderstanding, misuse of language or not being a genuine problem. For example, you deny that the situation or your misery is real. This could be because you're uncomfortable with uncertainty or because you desire stability above all else.

Accept. Acknowledging the paradox as an unresolved or potentially unresolvable issue within the current framework of understanding. For change/stability, you could acknowledge the paradox as a paradox without doing anything further. In this case you might think, 'That's the way it's always been. What can one person do? It's a strange world we live in.'

Resolve. Seek to dissolve the paradox by addressing its underlying causes. You might consider these approaches:

- Look at the underlying reasons for change and the desire for stability.
- Refine definitions. What does change mean to you? What about stability?
- Look at the conditions. How does constant change affect your well-being and the well-being of those around you? How much does it interfere with your external life? What about the desire for stability?
- Adjust the framework of understanding. For example, you might recognize that stability is not the absence of change, but a pattern of predictable changes. You might ask, what good is stability, if I am miserable or feel unfulfilled.
- Demonstrating how the apparent contradiction is only superficial (change and stability are the same thing to a differing degree) and can be reconciled by looking deeper at some of the answers or insights you have discovered. For example, you may maintain the stability of your current job, while laying a foundation for starting a business venture.

This approach can lead to creative thinking and insights to managing your perspective, attitude and behaviours.

Explore. Use the paradox as a catalyst for deeper inquiry and experience and to expand your perspective. This response offers the best opportunity for transformative growth.

* * *

Ultimately, the response to a paradox depends on personal inclinations, intellectual temperament and the specific nature of the paradox itself. Each response offers its own benefits and limitations, and individuals may employ different approaches depending on the context or paradox at hand. By engaging with paradoxes, we can broaden our understanding, stimulate critical thinking and navigate the complexities of the world with greater wisdom. The true choice available to us is to develop the steadiness of our inner minds while embracing the inevitability of external change.

Motivation Versus Inspiration

Being inspired is not enough. Motivation drives inspiration into action.

If you have a task that you must complete, you need the resources to accomplish that. Of these resources, motivation, which can be defined as a 'motive in action', is the most important. This driving force will help you achieve anything you aspire to, even in the face of obstacles. Motivation can help you persist and perform difficult tasks. No matter the goal you're working towards—health, career, relationship—you're driven by a motive. Every single goal has a reason behind it that compels you to act. For example, you may be inspired to build a website for your small business, but you should also feel motivated to complete it in a few months so you can move on to other projects and goals you need to take care of. While your level of inspiration may not have increased, postponing the completion of the website isn't an option, so motivation drives you to the finish line. This is an example of how motivation influences the outcomes of our lives.

Motivation and Inspiration: Definitions and Differences

While inspiration is *always* internal, motivation typically involves incentives, some of which are external. For example, you motivate a dog to learn a new trick by offering a treat at even the slightest effort towards the goal. You might motivate your children to finish their homework early by offering to increase their playtime if they do so.

You are inspired *to think* and motivated *to do*. You may be inspired when you read a quote on social media or a passage from a book that opens your mind and touches your heart. Words and images can trigger an epiphany that inspires you to think and then motivates you to act. What inspires you may touch your heart so deeply that it pulls you towards it. When this happens, we say it is a calling.

Inspiration often leads us to a creative place. The word inspiration, also considered 'divine guidance', comes from the Latin root verb *inspirare*, which means 'to breathe in'. Figurative definitions of inspiration include 'a breathing or infusion into the mind or soul'[1] or a 'special immediate action or influence of the Spirit of God (or of some divinity or supernatural being) upon the human mind or soul'.[2] Now you may wonder whether motivation is as great as inspiration or if one is simply a stepping stone to the other. Both inspiration and motivation are positive and necessary to living a life of purpose and excellence. Inspiration is comparable to the vision statement in a corporation and motivation to a mission statement.

Industrialist Henry Ford grew up on a farm. Many of the farmers in the area could not afford the expensive trucks needed to transport large quantities of their harvest to market. Their transportation challenges motivated Henry to ease their burden. He set out to manufacture a reliable mode of transportation that they could afford. Ford Motor Company's mission statement reflects his initial motivation: 'to make people's lives better by making mobility accessible and affordable'. Affordability was a challenge, but by implementing the assembly line, making automobiles became less expensive. When Ford was inspired to create this new kind of manufacturing process, he revolutionized travel and trucking for middle-class Americans. He provided the foundation for continually making smart vehicles for the smart world on a scale previously unimagined when he founded the company.[3]

Let me give you another example. Madame Curie was a Nobel Prize-winning physicist who coined the term radioactivity. Intrigued by the X-rays discovered by the German physicist Sir Wilhelm Röntgen and by Antoine Henri Becquerel's studies of phosphorescence and light absorption, she chose this new field of investigation for her thesis. She went on to discover radium and polonium and made many more significant contributions to the fields of chemistry and physics. Inspiration—a vague motivating feeling that propels us to explore the unknown—may have been the primary and deepest reason for Curie's ultimate success. The examples of Henry Ford and Madame Curie show that inspiration drives motivation and motivation drives perseverance and excellence. A clear vision drives a strong mission. Together, they are the driving forces for our chosen purpose in life.

Staying Motivated

Now, it is not possible for us to stay motivated or get inspired constantly. We *do* face rejections and failures along the way. How can we regain clarity and confidence and continue the journey towards our original purpose? Let me share a few tips for getting into the zone that fuels your inspiration or motivation.

1. **Recognize all those things that are already going well in your life.** This helps us develop a grateful, appreciative and positive attitude, which will de-stress our heart and unclutter our mind, leaving it relaxed, receptive and creative.

2. **Develop lateral thinking.** The ability to use an indirect, creative and imaginative method of solving problems is called lateral thinking. It involves 360-degree awareness and alertness.

3. **Observe the little things in life with wonder and appreciation.** We often say 'Don't sweat the small stuff.' We also say, 'Pay attention to details.' While the details are small and at times tedious, it is the small and simple things that inspire us the most. A grateful and awe-inspiring approach, which involves appreciating all that is wildly diverse around us, is both quite fascinating and a precursor for an inspired life.

4. **Develop motivation to inspire those you deeply care about,** such as a friend, colleague or relative. A long time ago, I read a quote from Booker T. Washington, an educator, author and reformer

who was born into slavery and became the most influential spokesperson for Black Americans between 1895 and 1915: 'The best way to lift oneself up is to help someone else.'[4] This is generosity. We never know the impact of a small act of kindness and generosity. It could trigger a great work of philanthropy helping millions of people. By putting a little bit of heart into our lives, our attitudes will change and we will embrace our society and humanity. That is the power of inspiration enabled by proper motivation.

5. **Daily meditation and introspection** will also provide the space in your heart for inspiration to sprout.

* * *

These tips will give you a good start. With constant exposure to inspiration, our motivations find refinement and expansion. In this journey of life, we can expand our perspective from 'me' to 'we' and 'mine' to 'ours' and begin to feel more connected to others. Then, like those renowned individuals who led inspired lives, such as Mother Teresa, Madame Curie and Martin Luther King, Jr., we too can make a significant difference to humanity. Motivated and inventive people such as Henry Ford, Alexander Graham Bell and Nikola Tesla improved the material well-being of generations and advanced our civilization. Why could you and I not do the same if we pursue our passions?

The clear distinction of inspiration is that it comes from the qualitative part of the heart that gives energy to the search for truth and betterment of life. The deeply motivated person acts on ideas that are essential for prosperity and progress for the self and others. However, being inspired is not enough, motivation is what drives inspiration to action. Constant inspiration and consistent motivation can help us achieve our purpose and find meaning in our lives.

Duty or Responsibility?

Duty entails responsibility. The one who has a duty must shoulder the responsibilities through which it is fulfilled.

One day, I was reflecting on the words 'duty' and 'responsibility', which, at the outset, appear to have similar meanings. However, looking deeper, I found profound nuances in their definitions that unlocked new insights.

Duties accompany the roles we take on, while responsibilities align with our aspirations. There is no love in fulfilling duties, yet with love present, carrying out responsibilities entailed in our duty can seem almost effortless. Responsibility is always expressed to some degree towards the self and is carried out voluntarily. This implies that a duty pertains to others and a responsibility to the self.

The paradox arises from the conflict between external obligations and the ability to act independently. How does the interconnectedness of duties and responsibilities shape individual actions and moral choices? Must we sacrifice our morals and actions for duty? Or can two complement each other? And if so, how?

Let us take a look at the duty of a crown prince, which is to prepare himself to become a king one day. His duties are preparing to serve and then serving the people. Whether he likes it or not, he is required by his family tradition to play his role in maintaining the rule. He will be forced into a lifetime of public service. That is the duty of the birth order in his family. His younger siblings will be spared having to take on this daunting duty unless the prince dies or resigns. Several princes in living memory have 'quit' the job and passed on the throne to the next in succession. They rejected family expectations.

What if the prince has an inner calling that differs from being a king? People's inner callings are different from the duties their families thrust upon them. Callings are very personal. If the inner calling of the prince is to become a saint, then the inner calling ultimately overpowers duty of the birth order. This is what happened in the life of Gautama Buddha. A calling is an ardent desire that will haunt us until we act upon it. It is our duty to ourselves to listen to our inner callings. Reflecting on this gave me the insight that we all have a duty by birth and a responsibility to an inner calling, which could also be called an *awakening*.

What do you think is the right thing to do in this situation? Should you follow the role within a societal or familial structure, or should you pursue a personal path (your calling) that might diverge radically from those expectations? Does true fulfilment come from adhering to externally imposed duties or from following a deeply personal responsibility to our own calling?

Each one of us has our own duties to perform. A crown prince prepares himself to be a king one day. Artists may paint, sculpt, make movies and so on, to develop their creative abilities and express the unique vision they see. The Bhagavad Gita calls for doing one's own duty, however simple it may be. The key words here are 'our own'. At times we may be enamoured by someone else's duty. Ruling a country must have its perks. We might then channel the enthusiasm we feel for their duty into overdoing our own duty or working hard for the sole purpose of future glory, long before we're ready for it. Yet, growth and glory lie in doing our *own* duty fully and completely in the present moment.

The idea that we can be fully engaged in duties and responsibilities without claiming any right to the outcomes, upends the conventional understanding of action and reward (act now for a future reward) and calls into question the very nature of effort, attachment and success.

How would jettisoning the conventional notion of action and reward change your decisions? What would you do differently as a result?

You may still be confused about the difference between duty and responsibility. So, let us reframe these two ideas.

Reframing Duty and Responsibility

The word 'duty' has its origins in the Latin root verb *debere* that means 'to owe'. Various people in our society dispense their duties because they believe they have a moral, ethical or logical debt to pay to someone. They commit to paying off the debt—that which is owed. There are many societal duties for everyone, such as the duty of citizens to adhere to the laws of the nation they reside in, which affords them benefits and protections.

The Latin root verb for responsibility is *respondere*, which means 'to respond'. The legal definition of the word *responsibility* is that one is 'liable', as in being liable for the damage you cause while crashing a car you're driving. In a courtroom, you would be a *respondent* to another person's claim that you owe them money for damages.

Another contemporary meaning of 'responsibility' is to 'act according to one's will without supervision'. This would refer to choosing to perform acts of altruism, such as working on behalf of the environment or at an animal shelter or volunteering for a non-profit. Although there is no legal obligation to do these things, it shows a high degree of personal evolution to perform self-selected responsibilities with joy.

The major difference I observe between duty and responsibility is that duty is assigned based on who we are or will become, whereas responsibility is something we choose to undertake of our own will. When we fulfil our responsibilities, we keep a promise. However, we could argue that duties and responsibilities are forms of service. In which case, both would be of equal importance. We could also consider that duty is the *what* and responsibility is the *how*.

In Sanskrit, the word *seva* means 'selfless service', or work performed without any thought of reward or repayment. In ancient India, seva was believed to help one's spiritual growth and at the same time contribute to the improvement of a community.[1]

Now, is one type of service higher or better than the other? Does it matter whether you're working towards equal rights to education, developing a vaccine, waiting tables, overseeing a construction crew, taking care of your grandmother or tending to your meditation practice? I'm afraid not. Duty entails responsibility. This may seem contradictory to what I've said so far but let me explain. Those who have a duty towards something must shoulder the responsibilities through which they fulfil the duty. When duty becomes a job or even a chore, it slips away from being responsible! The motivational speaker Zig Ziglar said, 'many quit working as soon as they find a job.' This is not being responsible in performing one's duty!

If a teacher accepts the duty to teach, she must fulfil numerous responsibilities—planning lessons, conducting classroom sessions, administering quizzes, grading papers, maintaining order, talking to parents—to ensure that she successfully performs her duty of teaching. While she may have a legal obligation—having signed a contract to provide these services—she could break her agreement or carry out her duty lazily. Through her dedication to teaching and her ethical desire to honour her commitment to her school, the teacher handles her responsibilities in a manner that ensures she successfully fulfils the duty of educating students.

Results without Attachment

In Sanskrit, the word for duty is dharma. The root of dharma is 'dhr', which means 'to uphold' or 'to support'. Uphold or support what? The truth, the good and the virtuous. Dharma means to uphold the truth and oppose the untruth. It means to support the good and eliminate the evil, to support the virtuous and defeat the unvirtuous. It also means that everyone is born with purpose and is expected to know and live for that purpose. Therefore, discernment (viveka) and focus (vairagya) are extolled as the prerequisite for, and virtuousness of, leading a fulfilling life of purpose.

In the Bhagavad Gita, Lord Krishna, as Arjuna's charioteer, inspires him to carry out his duty to fight the battle. This is an allegory for the battle to establish truth, goodness and virtue, and defeat deceit, evil and lack of virtue. This inspiring conversation between Krishna and Arjuna includes many of life's secrets, values and priorities, and results in the prince gaining sufficient clarity to pick up his weapon and fight.

The Bhagavad Gita encourages us to perform our duties in the correct spirit, with no attachment to the result. Krishna explains to Prince Arjuna that even when we perform our duties, we have no control over the results we get. And more profound is the lesson that we must not claim that we have any right to the results we are seeking.

Initially, this lesson could be a shock and unpalatable to you. It was for me. But on reflection, I understood that when we perform our duties with focus and clear intent, the results tend to be the best possible. Focusing on the end, without due consideration to putting in the best efforts, might come in the way of achieving the best result possible. There are also many factors outside our control that could affect the outcome. So how can we claim full right over results that are affected by many factors? The only thing we have control over is the preparation for and execution of our duty and its responsibilities.

If we become attached to results before they come to pass, we weaken our focus. If we are attached to the results after they are in, we might either gloat in success or feel depressed in failure. Both responses will dilute our character. So, there is wisdom in not being attached to or identifying with results. We focus on the goal from an aspirational perspective, that which is good for others or evolutionary for the self. Then, we do our best to engineer the best outcome. We are not what we achieve. We are not the glory that comes when our efforts succeed. We are not failures simply because our endeavours in a particular instance failed. External factors play an outsized role in both success and failure.

I believe that if, in our view, duties are as significant as personal callings, we will embrace our duties and perform them to the best of our ability. We will give them the same importance as our responsibilities, which are based on our choices and aspirations. We will be a happy parent, warrior or an employee as we wholeheartedly accept our duties and love to fulfil them. This approach is the key to inner harmony, peace of mind and happiness. You see, people sometimes feel guilty for choosing not to honour a duty that is imposed on them externally. But no one feels guilty for pursuing a calling that emanates from within.

In the Heartfulness school of thought, our primary duty as individuals is to recognize that we are spiritual beings having human experiences. Given this, the responsibility we choose includes doing all that we can to evolve and attain unconditional happiness through proper living.

Discipline Versus Regimentation

Discipline without love is incomplete. Complete discipline comes from within our heart and not from a rule or force outside us.

When I was growing up, we children were all loved and disciplined equally, one the same as another. Children invariably love to be spoilt with affection and attention from their parents, aunts and uncles but resent being disciplined. As I grew older and adopted a spiritual practice similar to the Heartfulness system of meditation, I learned the importance of discipline. Through regular practice, I benefited from discipline and understood its value.

Over the years, I have encountered many people who are disciplined, some perhaps more than myself. After a while, I began to wonder about such discipline. On closer observation, it occurred to me that sometimes discipline is a lot like regimentation—done by rote rather than driven by inner motivation. Think about exercise routines. We engage in them regularly to feel better, stay fit and improve our health. But often, our exercise becomes highly regimented. What happens if we slack off? We feel guilty for missing a few days. This does not feel good.

Feeling bad or guilty for missing a few workouts doesn't serve any purpose. After all, nothing remarkably terrible happens because we miss a few days of exercise at the gym, showing up for yoga class or even doing meditation.

Although the concepts of discipline and regimentation are closely related—both involve a form of control and order—they diverge in their approaches and implications for individual autonomy and creativity.

In my book *The Wisdom Bridge*, there's a section about disciplining your love rather than loving your discipline—'love' here being the affection you feel for and demonstrate to your children.[1] The same principle applies to your personal habits. Loving your discipline creates regimented thought and action, which can undermine the freedom discipline can lead to.

Regimentation

Regimentation is characterized by a lack of flexibility, and leading a regimented life is the result of being hard on yourself and others. It emphasizes uniformity, order and control, sometimes at the expense of individuality and personal freedom. The paradox within regimentation arises when the very structure meant to enhance efficiency and ensure consistency becomes a barrier to innovation, creativity and personal growth. While regimentation can create an environment of predictability and stability, it can also stifle the autonomy and flexibility necessary for individuals to explore new ideas, adapt to changes and express their unique talents and perspectives. There is no freedom in regimentation. Yet with discipline, it becomes a habit over time, leading to ease and comfort.

Being strict and regimented with yourself is one thing, but when you impose such rigidity on your children at home or your subordinates at work, the consequences can be even more detrimental. When you try to regiment the behaviour of others—your children, your partner, your co-workers—in time, they come to resent you. When you try to regiment your own behaviour—no matter the context—you risk burnout. Those who love discipline often expect everyone to follow strict regimentation in the name of it. They lose sight of the bigger picture. They lose perspective.

Understanding the difference between regimentation and discipline is more important when one takes up spiritual practice for personal development. In your spiritual practice, adopting rigid attitudes and strict routines can foster pride and other ego-driven expressions. Doing so prevents you from developing qualities essential to spiritual progress such as flexibility, generosity and humility.

Discipline

The purpose of discipline is to develop the capacity to do the right things correctly and with ease. Discipline is often self-imposed and revolves around self-control and the ability to pursue goals or adhere to personal values even though we might be tempted to abandon them. Discipline is a form of self-regulation that enables us to achieve long-term objectives and maintain good behaviour. Although discipline requires self-restraint—and often the temporary sacrifice of immediate pleasures or desires—it leads to greater freedom in the future, such as achieved goals, enhanced skills and the capacity to make wise choices. Through the constraint of discipline, we gain the freedom and ability to pursue a wider range of possibilities. However, the essence of true discipline extends beyond mere self-control.

Discipline without love is incomplete. True discipline comes from within your heart, not from an outside rule or force. You need to feel enthusiastic and inspired for discipline to last in any sphere, be it exercise or meditation. True discipline starts within you.

Self-discipline characterized by self-love is a form of governance. This means approaching activities like going to the gym or attending yoga class with the intention of loving and nurturing ourselves. It means settling in for our daily meditation because we are eager to increase our well-being. As we consistently pursue activities that are beneficial to us, many of those activities will become habits. When an activity becomes a habit, the burden of discipline falls away, and a natural flow emerges.

What makes discipline sustainable, and therefore useful, is not regimentation but flexibility. When we embrace flexibility, we open ourselves to the possibility of changing priorities with acceptance rather than self-recrimination, which enables us to pay full attention to them. Maintaining an attitude of flexibility and acceptance is critical in our relationships with others, especially with our spouses and children. Flexibility is of utmost importance for building, sustaining and deepening relationships.

Misinterpreting regimentation as discipline leads people to expect others to conform strictly to their own set of rules. This approach, whether employed by a teacher, coach or manager, can leave students, athletes and employees discouraged and uninspired. It also breeds disinterest in the programme and a high dropout or turnover rate.

Recent evidence shows that excessive training can lead to overuse injury, impaired well-being and decreased quality of life: 'Children and teens reap many physical and mental health benefits from participating in sports, but research shows about 70% of them drop out of these organized activities by age 13.'[2] So, it's critically important for teachers, coaches and bosses to understand the difference between discipline and regimentation.

The purpose of regimentation, whether inwardly or outwardly focused, is to establish strict control over behaviour and activities. By contrast, discipline is about capacity-building for the right behaviours. True discipline cultivates moderation in our external behaviours, enhancing our focus and clarity. It also helps us avoid rushing towards immediate gratification. The author of the bestselling book *Psycho Cybernetics*, Maxwell Maltz, is reputed to have said, 'The ability to discipline yourself to delay gratification in the short term in order to enjoy greater rewards in the long term is the indispensable requirement for success.'[3]

Regimentation and discipline can be distinguished by their essence. For example, democracy is inconsistent with regimentation. Franklin D. Roosevelt, the American President during World War II, famously said, 'They (who) seek to establish systems of government based on the regimentation of all human beings by a handful of individual rulers . . . call this a new order. It is not new and it is not order'.[4] Regimentation is mechanical, while discipline holds deeper meaning. Superficially, both words seem positive, promising strength, good health and success. However, comparing humans to machines doesn't resonate with our true nature. We are not robots, after all.

Strength is not found in rigidity but in flexibility. Whether we seek regimentation or discipline, we must incorporate a vital element to our approach: flexibility. It is flexibility that ensures the durability of our practices and empowers us to remain strong. It is the opposite of fragility.

A deep understanding of these nuances is critical for coaches, leaders and individuals engaged in integrated self-development programmes that include spiritual and contemplative practices. A contemplative practice is rooted in disciplined self-care that includes goal orientation, balanced emotions, self-love and self-compassion.

The Tolerance Paradox

In fact, tolerance is a bit like a ticking time bomb ready to explode if it is not backed by acceptance, emotional and intellectual maturity.

The night before his enlightenment, the soon-to-be Buddha meditated under the Bodhi tree, trying to reach Dharma or Truth. The Demon God Mara, the lord of death, wanted the seat of enlightenment for himself. Mara embodies desire, temptation and the obstacles that impede our path to enlightenment (desire, temptation, anger, lust, greed, doubt, pride, etc.). He challenged Siddhartha with everything he had. He sent his beautiful daughters to seduce him, demons to attack him, riches to taint him, and nothing worked. The Buddha continued to meditate, and every challenge transformed into flower petals and fell to the earth at his feet. At daybreak, Mara left in dismay just as the Buddha achieved enlightenment.

After that battle, the relentless Mara would visit the Buddha every so often, hoping to incite a confrontation. Every time Mara visited, despite the pure evil he represented, the Buddha would respond in a completely unexpected manner. He simply acknowledged the demon's presence and said very calmly, 'I see you, Mara. Come, join me for tea.'

Mara would drink his tea and slink off as always, disappointed about the lack of a reaction from the Buddha, who was not at all bothered by his presence.[1,2]

The story of Mara and Buddha illustrates how to manage life's challenges, no matter how great or small. Buddha maintained his focus, stayed true to the values that aligned with his purpose and acted with tolerance, acceptance, compassion and kindness. We can choose to do the same. Or we can choose to feel anger and act from rage, which can result in bad decisions, harm to ourself and others and lead to us falling off the righteous path and losing our way.

The paradox of tolerance examines both tolerance and acceptance, and between the two, challenges us to move beyond tolerance as the end goal and towards a deeper practice of acceptance that leads to love, understanding and inclusion, and eventually substantial and sustainable transformations.

First, let us look at tolerance.

Tolerance Defined

The concept of tolerance evokes mixed feelings for most of us. Imagine how you would feel if you were told that your presence was merely tolerated. You would likely feel unloved, deflated or even agitated. People like to feel loved, accepted and included, rather than simply tolerated, which is the first step. In broader contexts, a group or institution's commitment to tolerance can be essential to promoting equality and social justice.

Tolerance is the ability or willingness to allow the existence of ideas, opinions, practices and behaviours that differ from or conflict with our own. In some cases, tolerance involves putting up with people and things we perceive as wrong or unsuitable. These experiences, such as spending an entire family dinner seated next to a relative or we dislike, may be painful or abhorrent to us, but we tolerate them because saying how we genuinely feel would be rude. We also tolerate experiences we find uninteresting, such as completing a mandatory but boring task at work.

For example, your cousin could be singing karaoke, one song after another, at her birthday party. She may be an awful singer, but because singing brings her joy and it's her birthday, you tolerate the situation. If you are a good tolerator, you may even pretend to enjoy the singing. And you *do* enjoy seeing her happy. Tolerating situations of this type is fine.

On the other hand, people tolerate unbearable situations sometimes. We all know someone in our family, circle of friends or community who is in an abusive relationship where one partner tolerates the situation for the sake of young children or the stability of the family. Or we know someone who tolerates an abusive boss because the money is too good and their family needs the income.

Tolerance, however, does not require us to accept or adopt such behaviours ourselves. Tolerance, like any other attitude, must be applied appropriately. And in abusive situations, it isn't the best option, at least not for the long term. Tolerance is a bit like a ticking time bomb. We can only take so much before we explode. The exception is when our tolerance is built on a foundation of acceptance and emotional and intellectual maturity, which doesn't apply to situations where you're at risk.

Both Virtue and Vice

We need to be able to determine when tolerance is a virtue or a vice. It can be a virtue when it helps us to be less reactive to people, events and things we strongly dislike. As seen earlier, we might tolerate situations with families, friends and colleagues to maintain the status quo and avoid being rude. In these cases, tolerance is a virtue that can build compassion, kindness and acceptance. Tolerance can also increase our inner strength and courage. For example, a doctor might ask us to tolerate a measure of pain to avoid developing a reliance on medication.

Tolerance becomes a vice when it goes too far, such as when we overlook corrupt government officials, fail to prosecute known criminals or put up with situations that pose a threat to ourselves or others. I'm not sure it's virtuous for any wife to remain in an abusive relationship, believing herself to be 'a good wife' for doing so. Personal sacrifices of any kind are worthy only if they serve a higher purpose.

There is also a wrong understanding of religious scriptures when it comes to marriage and commitment. Marriage is supposed to happen in love, and no marriage should be tolerated under the circumstances of hate and abuse, irrespective of religious tradition or social mores.

Tolerating differences of opinion or cultural practices, however, has a strengthening effect. It is crucial for social harmony, peace and justice in our society. When we encounter a new culture, environment or social group, tolerance is essential for our survival. For example, in intercultural or interracial marriages, it is vital to tolerate the differences in cultural mores and practices. Tolerance serves as an internal buffer, increasing our resilience and reducing our vulnerability.

Inciting Change

It's important not to confuse tolerance with indifference or view it as an affirmation of what's being tolerated. Sometimes, courtesy requires us to acknowledge comments we do not like, such as a racial joke told by a co-worker, boss or client. However, our acknowledgement may be interpreted as our tolerance of such a behaviour. So, it is often better to remain silent or subtly express disapproval. The Buddha acknowledged and tolerated Mara when he visited. However, aside from offering tea, the Buddha ignored Mara's attempts to provoke him. Tolerance is an internal adjustment that makes us less reactive, allowing us a moment to adapt to or influence the transformation of others.

Although tolerance may not be considered a *great* virtue on its own, it is crucial to avoid intolerance. When intolerance prevails, violence is the consequence. Intolerance breeds anger and acts of violence that can be life threatening. Throughout history, nations have gone to war due to their inability to accept and appreciate the differences among people and their practices. Lack of understanding and appreciation of differences leads people to turn against one another. Intolerance—much like anger—should be directed only at ourselves for the purpose of self-improvement. Even then, it's advisable to approach self-correction and the resolve to change with compassion.

Tolerance is not a virtue when we face unacceptable situations where our active involvement can bring about transformation. Two examples that come to mind are climate change and the institution of family.

When it comes to climate change, our society's constant adjustments to a deteriorating environment have brought us to the brink of crisis. Temperatures are rising. So are our oceans. Drought is increasing. Storms occur more frequently and are more destructive than ever. On an average, 23.1 million people were displaced per year during 2010–19. Thirteen million people die each year from the impacts of climate change. The United Nations has declared climate change the 'single biggest health risk facing humanity'.[3]

People living longer and having fewer children has led to a greater proportion of elderly (aged sixty-five and above) in the population.[4] This raises a fundamental concern because the continuity of our way of life relies on a balanced population distribution of age, talent and occupation. Economic mobility can disrupt family dynamics causing stress and anxiety (downward mobility) or altering roles and responsibilities which increases the pressure to maintain new social standards (upward mobility). It can also contribute to generational tensions, as those moving up may adopt new values or lifestyles that differ from their elders. Then there is all the outside noise families live with—the overwhelming presence of social media and news—that discourages them from doing things together and communicating with each other. The constant noise in their world hinders the development of values and qualities necessary for a better and happier life. Residing in predominantly nuclear families far-flung from our elders, we no longer have the benefit of their wisdom, love and support. We need to seek the wisdom of our elders and learn from their experience. When we integrate this wisdom into our modern lifestyle, we will be able to navigate life's challenges better.

Tolerating these concerning trends in climate change and family dynamics stems from indifference and apathy, which are poor attitudes towards these critical life issues. At some point, enough becomes enough. Excessive tolerance inevitably invites its opposite and sparks a movement characterized by intolerance. This is because with excessive tolerance people may begin to feel that boundaries are being ignored or that permissiveness allows harmful behaviours to flourish, which can lead to a backlash aimed at restoring order or control. History has shown that societies can pivot and bring about transformative change.

Non-Violent Social Change

The Indian independence movement, led by Mahatma Gandhi, aimed to secure civil rights and self-governance for Indians under British colonial rule. His non-violent approach to political change has influenced civil disobedience movements around the world, including in South America, the US and Africa. In 1947, the movement culminated in India's independence, granting civil rights to the people of India. The Indian Constitution was adopted in 1950, which provided a legal framework to protect these rights.

The decades that followed the 1950s civil rights movement in the United States prompted enormous change for the improvement of the lives of African Americans and women in the workplace. The Civil Rights Act ushered in the possibility of minorities owning homes and accessing higher education more easily. The Act attempted to level the playing field and made the discriminatory practices in bank lending and admission to elite schools and work illegal. Today, this Act has helped the country become more successful, open and diverse. When tolerance reaches its limits, a positive and necessary change is forthcoming.

Meaningful change begins with the choices we make for ourselves. If we try to control other people, we end up being oppressive. Tolerance isn't relevant when it comes to people and situations beyond our control and influence. It's better to live and let live. If we have no choice but to be with a specific group of people, such as our family members, it's best to cultivate acceptance based on love and understanding.

While tolerance often requires patience and adaptation, acceptance requires only love and a non-judgemental attitude. Acceptance allows our relationships to be flexible and focused on growth.

Love is the bedrock of non-judgemental and cheerful acceptance. In any relationship, love is the most effective solution for resolving conflicts and finding common ground. It has the power to dissolve problems and serve as a catalyst for positive transformation, which, over time, inspires progress.

The way we need to understand the role of tolerance, similarly, we also need to understand what acceptance means. Acceptance is not passively waiting for miracles to happen. Instead, it provides a foundation for initiating change. It does not absolve us of responsibility or relinquish our ability to make things better. Acceptance facilitates understanding of both our own situations and those of others. With this understanding, change is possible. Thus, acceptance is a prerequisite for initiating change. The relationship between tolerance and acceptance is that we can tolerate without accepting, but we cannot accept without tolerating.

When we truly understand acceptance and tolerance, we then appreciate the need to develop acceptance and concern for certain vital aspects of life. How can tolerance be justified in situations such as family disintegration and child poverty? Robust families and well-nourished thriving children are vital to societal well-being. Tolerance should be reserved for 'bad' things. There's no effort or internal gymnastics required to embrace 'good' things. For example, few need to tolerate eating ice cream on a hot summer day— they simply enjoy it. We only tolerate cold when we shiver or heat when the weather is sweltering. This demonstrates that tolerance is for transient elements around us. The danger of excessive tolerance is feeling trapped in a state of helplessness and forgetting how capable we are to create a new life for ourselves. This excessive tolerance is not a good mental state to be in.

When we mistakenly tolerate people and love material things, we often get it wrong. But when we discern between people, events and things, and calibrate our emotional connection accordingly, we can learn to accept people and engage with events, while tolerating temporary things and situations. By accepting people as they are, our tolerance of them is encompassed within that acceptance. Acceptance of people usually exudes love and that becomes an agent of change and transformation.

So let us cheerfully accept rather than merely tolerating the pain, suffering and the perceived 'shortcomings' of those who differ from us in appearance or thinking. This acceptance naturally paves the way to improve things for everyone. In that sense, acceptance is dynamic. Without wholeheartedly accepting our current circumstances, change cannot take place. This type of acceptance evolves into understanding and appreciation of differences, which fosters sustainable change.

Unless we can understand people whose views and values counter ours, we cannot hope to help them shift their views and behaviour, or ours for that matter, if needed. I am reminded of the words attributed to Theodore Roosevelt: 'No one cares how much you know until they know how much you care.' Caring can affect huge change. Acceptance, understanding and appreciation are all part of caring. Tolerance falls short in conveying the depth of caring that is involved in practising kindness and compassion. These two qualities arise out of acceptance.

The Stillness Paradox

If you would like to develop stillness deliberately, I suggest you practice being quiet. Simply sit in silence and do nothing. That is, if you can.

How can we become still amidst the noise of the world? It may seem challenging, but it is possible. While it's true that we must rest after a long day, many of us struggle to keep our minds calm and experience restful sleep even when we're feeling tired. Insomnia robs us of the rejuvenating rest we need. The lack of stillness in our hectic lifestyles has led to ever-wandering minds and fidgety bodies.

Stillness is crucial for developing the ability to observe, focus and effectively perceive and understand what we encounter. It is also essential for developing intuition by listening to the constant guidance from our heart; it is always talking, we just need to listen. Therefore, we must be mindful of anything that disturbs our stillness such as noise. By its very nature, noise, which is created by a discordance in sound waves, [1] lacks organization and disrupts our tranquillity.

The Wandering Mind

The noise in the external world can distract us and pollute our minds, dulling our senses. Moreover, the internal noise of unruly and undisciplined streams of thought can hinder our mental clarity and become an emotional burden. These unruly thoughts resemble the cacophony of discordant sounds. Just as noise disturbs and pollutes the atmosphere, unruly thoughts can be considered internal noise pollution that affect the mind. When this kind of unruly thinking becomes habitual, it disrupts the mind, causing confusion and chaos. It dulls the mind and can contribute to mental illness.

To prioritize our overall health, especially our mental well-being, we must experience a period of stillness each day. Similar to sleep, stillness allows our physical systems to rejuvenate and our minds to process our experiences.

If you would like to cultivate stillness deliberately, I recommend practising silence. Simply sit quietly and do nothing. This can be challenging for many individuals. When asked to sit and quiet their minds, they find soon themselves getting up and walking away as a whirlwind of thoughts inundates their minds. Initially, sitting in stillness may seem to bring more chaos to our minds compared to when we're moving around. This is because the mind now turns its focus on itself, away from the external senses of sight, smell, taste, touch and sound. In which case, the solution to our distractions may seem worse than the problem itself.

When the mind focuses outwards, it can more clearly absorb and process external stimuli or impressions from the world. The reverse is also true. When the mind turns inwards, it becomes more aware of its own nature—specifically, that it is constantly generating thoughts based on the impressions it has received from the outside. In other words, focusing outwards helps the mind understand external reality, while focusing inwards helps it understand its own processes and how it creates thoughts.

The mind wanders from thought to thought. If the nature of the thought is heavy, the mind worries. If the nature of the thought is a desire, the mind plans how to fulfil that desire. So goes the wandering mind. But there's no need to worry; you can cultivate stillness through practice.

While a few of us are born with the ability to be still and see our mental activity clearly, the rest of us need to develop this skill.

Holistic Stillness

The state of stillness encompasses both the body and mind, and we must cultivate both aspects to achieve true stillness. The physical, mental and emotional aspects of our existences are interconnected. Some people manifest their wandering or restless mind through physical restlessness, while a calm mind is reflected in graceful movement. Similarly, emotional confusion can be clear on our faces: we frown, our mouths drop open and we may even squint.

The relationship between our physical, mental and emotional states extends further into the spiritual realm. A comprehensive spiritual practice involves nurturing a supple and flexible body through yoga postures and breathing exercises, cultivating non-judgemental awareness and focusing the mind on higher ideals. When our mental and emotional states are confused or fatigued, walking briskly in nature triggers the release of happy hormones that have a positive effect on our mood. Similarly, relaxation and meditation provide physical energy, rejuvenate the mind and make us feel calm and happy.

While yoga is commonly known for its physical benefits, it also offers a path to stillness. To develop our ability to be still, we need to find the causes of our restlessness and address them. Mental and emotional restlessness may arise from the difficulty of managing worry, stress and unfulfilled desires, as well as a lack of effective planning to reach a goal.

In Heartfulness, the practices of relaxing, meditating, rejuvenating (cleaning) and connecting to the inner self influence emotional, mental and physical stillness. Heartfulness relaxation is a method that relaxes our body and mind by drawing on the autogenic (self-generated) capability of the body–mind complex. By visualizing a tranquil environment and focusing on regulating our breathing, our heart rate slows, inducing a state of calmness.[2] You can also relax your body one section at a time, from the tips of your toes to the top of your head, for the same effect. Through meditation, we develop our ability to focus on a single thought. We train ourselves to ignore the wandering mind; this, over time, leads to mental and emotional stillness.

The Settled Mind

While it may not be possible to free ourselves entirely from worry and stress, we can build the capacity to manage them effectively. Feeling stressed shows that we have exceeded our capacity to manage emotions, tasks, input from the environment and so on. Not being able to manage our responsibilities is a sign of being overwhelmed with worry, which can erode the confidence that lies at the base of our physical, mental and emotional capacities.

The practice of pausing for introspection, visualization and contemplation helps us deal with our stress by allowing us to temporarily park our worries. When meditation is practised correctly, we feel more settled in our thinking, and this feeling of tranquillity then permeates our minds and bodies.

The great yogi Ram Chandra of Fatehgarh (affectionately known as Lalaji) said, 'it is the settledness of the mind on a subject that brings happiness. If that settledness is not there, then you will be jumping from one thing to another without any resolution. You will not have any closure, you will not have any satisfaction, and you will not have any peace. You will still be vacillating and dissatisfied all your life, and you will not have learned anything from all your activities.'[3]

Being settled does not imply inactivity; rather, it signifies operating at a level of engagement and focus we may never have even conceived of. Whether studying a subject, pursuing a business venture or addressing a challenging situation, our minds should remain steady and attentive, no matter what we're doing. A steady, focused mind doesn't mean that we are fully attentive to one thing and less attentive to another. Having multiple concerns in life should not diminish our mental abilities.

The idea behind all yogic practices is to make the mind still and steady. Such a mind will exude 360-degree awareness and alertness. Dr Richard Davidson, a researcher at the University of Wisconsin, studied the brains of long-term 'Olympic' meditators (those who have meditated 62,000 hours in their lifetime) and found that they reach higher levels of brain activity, as indicated by gamma waves recorded by an electroencephalogram (EEG). These individuals also exhibit enhanced focus and flow, exemplifying the harmonious integration of stillness and activity.[4]

'Gamma brain waves have the highest frequency among all brain waves. They are associated with high levels of thought and focus . . . Studies have also revealed that increased gamma brain wave activity can help you achieve the highest concentration levels. Gamma waves can also promote higher states of awareness and increased brain function during meditation.' Gamma waves improve cognition, problem-solving ability, information processing and memory; increase awareness and mindfulness; and boost the brain's immunity and function.[5] Research shows that any meditation practice increases gamma waves, and the longer you practise, the greater the effect. By practising stillness, we can tap into the power of gamma waves and experience its benefits. The ability to achieve stillness and cultivate a focused mind not only supports our meditation practice but also improves our overall effectiveness.

Harmony in Discord

Let us say that we accept yoga and meditation as ways to quieten noise. Yet, as a paradox, how do we solve the contrast? We could reject the noise as not existing, claiming that it's become such a part of our lives that we no longer hear it. Or we might reject the ill effects of that noise. Or we might fully accept the havoc that noise can create on our systems and flee to a cave to avoid it altogether. However, what if we embraced the noise as part of life, a piece of the whole? What if we explored the spaces underneath and around the symphony of noise to find the quiet melody of stillness within the discord?

We might think of life as a symphony of discordant notes. Yet, if we listen with our hearts, we can detect the quiet melody of stillness within. This stillness is not an absence of noise. No. It is a presence, or fullness, that dwells at the heart of noise. Just as courage is not the absence of fear but the ability to overcome fear, stillness is not the absence of noise but the ability to transcend noise. That way, we can place our focus where it's needed to achieve what we need to achieve.

Another way of looking at the stillness paradox is to appreciate that we could stand still on the earth, which is mostly still and silent at night, while moving through space at a tremendous speed. The same holds true for a top that's spinning so fast that it seems not to be moving at all. Theoretically, if we were to keep pace with the speed of light, even time comes to a standstill. So, there is so much speed and activity and yet stillness. How is this possible in the mundane world? Is this possible in the spiritual or metaphysical realm? Only in thought can we move at the speed of light. Only in thought we can be with others irrespective of the distance or time or circumstances. We will explore the power of thought as the resolution of the stillness paradox as we explore the ideas of thinking and remembering later in this book.

Part 2

Emotions and Relationships

The Child Is Father of the Man

The children who have a wonder-filled outlook towards the world and their place in it will evolve into adults who appreciate and respect the wonder that is nature.

When a phrase sounds contradictory, as paradoxes do, digging deeper into its essence can open worlds of questions, insights and new perspectives, which prompt more questions, insights, and on it goes. These seeming contradictions turn up in poems and texts of ancient wisdom, where they serve as a map, a shortcut or an entrance to the worlds that lie within the contradictions. They open us to realizations that the words alone might not or cannot capture. The line 'The Child is Father of the Man' from William Wordsworth's poem 'My Heart Leaps Up' (1807) is one such powerful contradiction. It is a curious reversal of what we know about where babies come from, and this piques our interest.

Wordsworth wrote:
My heart leaps up when I behold
A rainbow in the sky:
So was it when my life began;

> So is it now I am a man;
> So be it when I grow old,
> Or let me die!
> The Child is Father of the Man;
> And I could wish my days to be
> Bound each to each by natural piety.[1]

What does this mean, the child is the father of the man? How is the child the parent of an adult? The poem implies that who we are as children lays the foundation of who we are as adults. Our adulthood is born out of our experiences and perceptions as children. The paradox is that instead of fathers teaching their acquired wisdom to their children, their children have something to teach them. This concept challenges our linear perceptions of time and growth, opening the door into the unknown even wider, and this is the result of feeling a sense of awe in nature.

When we take a moment to allow ourselves to be touched by the spirit of the words in the poem— embracing the wondrous child within, stepping on to the porch or standing atop a hill, gazing at the sky or the vast landscape—we may find ourselves filled with gratitude and wonder. In these moments, we can feel the profound interconnectedness of life and gain a renewed reverence for nature. Regardless of age, nature brings joy to our hearts.

Although the capacity for awe is inherent in all of us, this wonder is deeply spiritual and personal. Perhaps, this is why Wordsworth expresses his desire for each day to be infused with the same 'natural piety', the exultation the speaker experiences when seeing the beauty of a rainbow. As one commentator points out, 'The words "natural piety" imply that the speaker considered this feeling for nature to be so reverent that seeing a rainbow is an almost spiritual experience.'[2]

Spirituality and Nature

William Wordsworth and Samuel Taylor Coleridge launched the English Romantic movement (1778–1837) with the 1978 publication of their book of poetry, *Lyrical Ballads*, three years after the Bhagavad Gita was first published in English (1775). Since then, numerous studies have established the influence of Indian thought on the Romantic poets,[3] whose works are layered with concepts of karma, the universal soul, the divine in nature, immortality and reincarnation.[4]

Wordsworth's views on spirituality and nature were greatly influenced by Hinduism.[5] The Romantic poets believed that 'Nature was infused with the divine soul. Nature was transfigured into a living force held together as a unity by the breath of the divine spirit'.[6] The speaker in 'My Heart Leaps Up' diligently hopes not to lose this natural piety or sense of the divine presence in the natural world, no matter how old he becomes. Without this sense of the divine, the speaker would rather die.

Both the Bhagavad Gita and 'My Heart Leaps Up' suggest that a sense of wonder can lead to spiritual insight and a deeper understanding of the universe's nature. Awe and wonder can manifest as a sense of peace, purpose and connection to something greater than oneself. Both texts suggest that this sense of wonder is key to understanding deeper truths about existence. While the Gita approaches this through a spiritual and philosophical dialogue—highlighting the soul's immortality and the nature of the divine—Wordsworth's poem celebrates the beauty of the natural world and its capacity to inspire a sense of wonder that connects us to the larger truths of life.

What prevents us from experiencing such a reverent sense of interconnectedness throughout the day or in other settings? Is it our adult personalities? How important is childhood in shaping who we become? How can we hold on to that feeling as adults?

Maintaining Innocence and Wonder

Our adult personality is shaped by the combination of our childhood temperament and the environment in which we grow up. Until about the age of five, we are highly impressionable. While we possess innate abilities that help us process information and instinctively respond to our environment, it is through interpreting the world that we begin to lose our inherent purity and innocence.

If we continue to immerse ourselves in an environment of natural wonder, where observation, experience and learning are positive, we can maintain that naturalness. Yet even if we didn't have the privilege of such an environment during our childhood, neuroplasticity allows us to develop that sense of wonder later in life. This presents a paradox between the seemingly permanent effects of upbringing and the brain's ability to change and adapt, suggesting that our essence is both malleable and enduring.

When I read this poem, I contemplated the psychological wisdom in the idea of a child being the father of a man, the importance of sowing seeds of goodness and purity in future generations, and my own childhood experience of gazing at a rainbow with awe and wonder. As an adult, I still feel the same sense of awe. This awe connects me to my favourite memories of myself as a pure, innocent child marvelling at the wonder of creation.

How can we help our children retain their innate sense of pure naturalness? How can we reconnect to the wonder, curiosity, kindness and goodness that were inherent in our childhood essence? These virtues, inspired by our reverence for the divine in nature, hold great significance and should be cherished and passed along. The parent and child within us are one and the same. By lovingly tilling the soil and sowing the right seeds at the right time in our inner child, we can embrace the notion of parenting ourselves. We can perhaps deliberately embark on a journey back to simplicity, purity and wonder.

Despite its tricky phrasing, the simple, heartful observation that children's wonder about the world and their place in it helps them evolve into adults who genuinely value and honour the wonder of nature, is not a contradiction. Thus, the parent who carries the eternal sense of wonder and appreciation for the magnificent world surrounding them is none other than the child herself. A parent who is filled with wonder is a magnificent child of creation!

The Passion Paradox

Passion could be the link between love and anger. So, how do we refine our passion so that there is more love and less anger?

Swami Vivekananda, a spiritual genius and one of the most inspiring intellectual forces behind India's freedom movement, advocated for physical, mental and spiritual freedom. He said, 'No great work can be achieved by humbug. It is through love, a passion for truth, and tremendous energy, that all undertakings are accomplished.'[1] Although he cited passion as crucial for achieving goals, he also said, 'One may gain political and social independence, but if one is a slave to his passions and desires, one cannot feel the pure joy of real freedom.'[2] In other words, the same passion that fuels the drive towards our goals can be both productive and destructive, leading to endless seeking, suffering and burnout on a personal level. It all depends on how we channel that drive.

Creative and Constructive Passion

Passion has the power to push us towards our goals no matter the obstacles. Vincent van Gogh, who painfully struggled with mental illness, expressed his passion for art and his profound relationship with nature into some of the world's greatest masterpieces. He found excitement, solace and healing in the process: 'I cannot,' he wrote to his brother, Theo, 'suffering as I am, do without something that is greater than I am, which is my life, the power to create.'[3] Through his art, he channelled that something greater, and in turn, that something greater and his gift for capturing it, opens the hearts, minds and spirits of those who view his work.

Passion is a source of personal fulfilment. It is also a catalyst for innovation, discovery and social change. When people are deeply passionate about their endeavours, they can overcome obstacles, inspire others and make a lasting impact on the world.

Marie Curie's passion for science and dedication to research led to the discovery of radioactivity, as well as laying the foundation for future research in nuclear physics and cancer treatment. Her example shows how passion can fuel discovery and contribute significantly to human knowledge and well-being.

Malala Yousafzai's passion for education and belief in the right of every child to receive one have made her a global symbol of peaceful resistance against the suppression of children's and young people's rights to education. From Malala's story, we see how passion can inspire a global movement and bring about significant social change.

Steve Jobs's passion for design and innovation exemplifies how passion can drive someone to challenge the status quo, inspire others and create products that change the world.

Passion not only plays a crucial role in huge achievements but also significantly impacts our everyday lives, driving personal growth, fulfilment and positive change. It drives each and every one of us—entrepreneurs, humanitarians, artists, teachers, parents, activists—everyone, whatever our passion, however we best express it. This is the positive side of passion.

I know many of you can think of times when passion drove creative thoughts and inspired action. What about those times? What did you learn from them? Or what could you learn?

When Passion Becomes Destructive

Passion, while a powerful and often positive force, can have its downsides. Those motivated by passion may sometimes become angry or forceful, lacking the necessary discernment to harness their passion to achieve good and great things. When this passion is expressed as anger and rage, it becomes negative and destructive. People of good conscience, who strive for non-violence, may cause others to feel dismayed by their angry outbursts, which might involve raised voices or hurtful remarks that inflict emotional wounds on others. Such anger-filled reactions harm our intimate relationships. Loved ones want to stay away from us and relationships fall apart.

Steve Jobs, known for his intense passion for perfection in Apple's products, sometimes allowed this passion to manifest in ways that were challenging for those around him. His high standards and demanding nature led to significant innovations but also strained relationships with colleagues and employees. This example illustrates how an unbridled passion for excellence, without the balance of empathy and understanding, can lead to interpersonal conflicts and emotional depletion.

People driven by passion may find themselves obsessed with achieving their goals, driving themselves until they're completely drained. They can become addicted to the rush of adrenaline. Individuals in high-performance careers (such as healthcare, law and tech start-ups) often have a deep passion for their work and a desire to make an impact. However, without proper boundaries and self-care, this passion can lead to burnout—a state of physical, emotional and mental exhaustion caused by prolonged stress, skipping meals, not getting enough sleep and putting loved ones and other commitments on the back burner.

Just as I know many of you have experienced the constructive power of passion, I am equally sure many of you have let your passions take over, causing burnout in school, work and at home. You may have become frustrated or angry and lashed out. You may have drained all your energy. What were the warning signs? How might you learn to observe those signs in the future? What might you do differently to avoid blow-ups or burnout?

Anger is a natural human emotion and can be directed constructively when purpose takes precedence and anger becomes a tool for achieving that purpose in an ordered and moderate way. This is especially true when the purpose is to right wrongs done to others. Mahatma Gandhi, the Reverend Martin Luther King, Jr., and Malala Yousafzai all advocated non-violence when protesting injustice. While anger can be a powerful motivator for change, fuelling passion in social and political movements, it can also lead to destructive outcomes when not channelled constructively; it undermines the very goals it seeks to achieve.

In his sermon 'Loving Your Enemies', Martin Luther King, Jr., spoke out against the violence of the death penalty: 'Darkness cannot drive out darkness,' he said, 'only light can do that. Hate cannot drive out hate; only love can do that.'[4]

Our emotions are built on top of and mixed with other emotions, which makes them complicated to manage. For example, if anger becomes entangled with fear, insecurity or inferiority, controlling that anger becomes extremely challenging. Usually, the outcomes are quite disproportionate to the immediate trigger that caused our anger.

Suppose you are afraid of losing your job. You've been managing your interactions with your boss carefully and suppressing your anger or frustration for a long time. Until one day you either can't take it any more or you lose all hope of keeping your job and can no longer suppress your feelings. This is where you should take a moment, because all that anger you've been holding in could just explode.

The Antidote to Anger Is Love

When we feel our anger or frustration rising, it is crucial for us to pause, reflect on the cause of our anger and, with that understanding, realign the passion and its direction with the goal of being open-hearted in embracing that situation with grace, understanding and creativity. Once the intensity of our anger or the urgency to express it subsides, we can communicate with others in a non-threatening manner.

If our intentions are pure, we can take corrective action. Fortunately, through gentle and loving introspection, we can moderate anger. By pausing and reflecting, we can cultivate a perspective on approaching people, events and obstacles with greater kindness, compassion and love. In doing so, we discover the true essence of spiritual growth and enlightenment. Self-awareness is a powerful tool for transforming our behaviour in any context. So, it becomes essential to refine our passion and cultivate a greater abundance of love while minimizing anger, frustration or excessive work. Love is the antidote.

Love is often associated with tender and affectionate emotions we reserve for our families and loved ones. It has a profound ability to deeply nurture everything that springs forth from us, including passion. We also know that passion can be expressed through acts of love, whether these acts occur in the context of a relationship or in the pursuit of our callings. Love enables us to forge meaningful connections with others, acting as the fuel that drives our relationships and endeavours.

Without love's ennobling energy and positive force, many of life's loftiest purposes would remain unfulfilled. Contrary to popular belief, love is not something we receive or give—it is an inherent part of our being. Love goes beyond sentiment. Its nurturing essence permeates everything we do, providing the foundation for our actions and relationships. It makes human connections possible. However, it's important to recognize that we can love others only as much as we love ourselves. By embracing this deeply nurturing ability, we can turn love into a catalyst for passion, infusing all that we do with purpose and vitality.

Transforming Anger to Love

Passion is also a physical experience in addition to being an emotional one. Interestingly, when we are in love or in anger, we can feel those emotions viscerally in our hearts. The beating of our hearts quickens or the heart skips a beat, signalling that something meaningful is taking place. In these moments, we feel alive. Perhaps, the goal is to develop a compassionate and discerning heart, one that channels passion into positive action, one that is creative and ennobling rather than one that intentionally or unintentionally causes harm.

Anger, when refined through introspection, can be transformed into expressions of love. How does this work? A regular practice of yoga and meditation can help you stay calm and relaxed, stay centred in your heart and open yourself to differences and possibilities. Yoga brings about overall health. The purpose of yoga is not just physical health through *asanas* (body postures) and *pranayamas* (breathing exercises), it also establishes rich spiritual insight within us.

How we channel our passion is up to each of us. We always have control over our emotions and actions. Always. Although it might not always feel that way. When you feel that you're close to losing control, giving yourself two minutes between the inclination to express your anger in a non-productive manner and doing so, as well as shifting yourself through rightful yogic practices into love, will be a wonderful intervention. You'll be able to maintain your inner cool, sense of calm and unity. You'll feel compassion towards the individual or individuals who triggered your anger. Isn't that wonderful? You'll not only maintain your cool, but you'll establish a better relationship with yourself and with those around you. For that, we need to mediate. The meditative mind can be very powerful.

It is crucial to remember that by refining the entire complex of our emotions, we develop clarity, confidence, courage, calmness and contentment—qualities that bring about a strong transformation within us.

Cultivating these qualities that bring about transformation is possible for everyone. With a commitment to a daily practice of Heartfulness, anyone can develop a non-judgemental awareness and a perceptive heart.

The Desire Paradox

A really happy person is one who is happy under all circumstances.

We all want to be happy. The right to the pursuit of happiness is enshrined in the Constitution of the United States of America and the founding documents of many other democratic countries. In 2011, the United Nations adopted a resolution that identified the pursuit of happiness as 'a fundamental human goal' and, in the following year, declared 20 March as the International Day of Happiness. Bhutan prioritizes gross national happiness (GNH), which is measured by their gross national happiness index over gross domestic product (GDP). But what makes us happy? Is the aim of these resolutions and proclamations to promote economic and personal well-being by providing relief from pain and poverty, thus creating the conditions for happiness? Do economic security and a life free from pain really make us happy? I'm not sure they do. Indeed, they reduce stress and increase comfort and well-being, yet improving external circumstances alone is insufficient.

My spiritual guide Ram Chandra of Shahjahanpur, affectionately known as Babuji, used to say that a truly happy person is one who is happy under all circumstances.

How is this possible? It would be possible only if happiness were unconditional. To be happy under all circumstances involves finding happiness within yourself, just as you are, without relying on external conditions. In this life, we will experience unpleasant circumstances. And it is extremely difficult to attain this state of mind of being happy under all circumstances.

None of us seek misery. However, when we do get our share of it, what do we do? Babuji said that a life without suffering and misery is 'impossible and unnatural. In fact,' he said, 'they are rather meant for our betterment'.[1]

> They are just like bitter pills of medicine given to a patient to restore health. The misuse of even the best thing creates trouble. So is the case with miseries. Proper utility of everything at the proper time and in the proper way is sure to bring forth good results in the long run. Miseries are really our best guide, which make our path smooth. To a man in the ordinary sphere of life, miseries are very helpful for his making . . . In fact, to put up coolly with miseries and troubles contributes much to our betterment; hence they are valuable assets to our progress. It is only by their wrong use that we spoil their effect and thus get deprived of their best advantages.[2]

We all seek security, comfort and happiness because we are hardwired for them. However, when we seek happiness in things, events and people, we are missing the point. We are making happiness conditional. If that is the situation, no wonder, even with all the resolutions and proclamations, there is so much unhappiness in the world.

Getting to Zero

Why do we go after acquiring things and achieving results? Careful observation shows that some people are happy with less, while others continue to feel unhappy even though they have more. From this observation, we can easily conclude that happiness is not dependent upon the things we possess or the successes we have accumulated. Many feel unhappy despite chasing their desires and fulfilling an ever-increasing number of them.

Our attachment to and constant focus on what we desire *increases* stress. We become anxious that we won't achieve what we desire, and when we do, after our initial pleasure, our happiness level returns to what it was before the achievement. And what happens then? Do we rest? Do we give ourselves a break? No. We set another goal to achieve yet another desire. It is exhausting and stressful, this unceasing pursuit of more and the accompanying anxiety that more will never be enough. Desire always leaves us wanting more. No wonder happiness eludes most of us.

The nineteenth-century German philosopher Arthur Schopenhauer thought of happiness 'as a lasting satisfaction of all desires'.[3] By his definition, the happiness of a person can be described mathematically as follows: Happiness = Number of desires fulfilled/Total number of desires.

According to this equation, if you have ten desires and five are fulfilled, your happiness equals 50 per cent. If all ten desires are fulfilled, your level of happiness is 100 per cent. The caveat is that the more desires you have, the harder it will be to fulfil all of them, so if you continue creating new desires, you will be less happy. Therefore, happiness becomes inversely related to the number of desires, because fulfilling more and more of them becomes less likely.

Consider what would happen if you eliminated your desires until you had none? The denominator in the equation would become zero. Anything you divide by zero equals infinity. Therefore, if you have zero desires, you will be infinitely happy. Limitlessness will be your source of happiness. In the Bhagavad Gita, when Arjuna asks Lord Krishna the formula for happiness, Lord Krishna says, 'Just as the ocean remains undisturbed by the incessant flow of river waters merging into it, likewise the sage—who is unmoved despite the flow of all desirable objects all around him—attains peace, and not the person who strives to satisfy desires.'[4]

My view of happiness as unconditional is bound to disappoint some people. Wouldn't it be impractical not to have, let alone try to satisfy, any desires at all? Wouldn't desires motivate us to do better and help others? You wouldn't want to eliminate those outcomes, would you?

Fulfilling duties and responsibilities towards others should not be confused with desires that are multiplied in the pursuit of ego gratification. For the sake of simplicity in this discussion, let us agree to view desires as coming from the perspective of the gratification of the ego. So, with each desire, we seed discontent in our heart and, as a result, happiness is harder to achieve. Cultivating a joyful and contented heart is a better route to happiness.

And what is joy if not happiness? Don't we feel joyful when we are happy and vice versa? Why seek happiness if we are really in need of joy? The simple difference is that when we seek happiness, we focus on the acquisition of things, including praise and recognition. Orientation towards status and approval results in leading a competitive lifestyle instead of living contentedly. It invariably results in feelings of hurt, isolation and unhappiness. Seeking joy has an inward focus.

Joy can be defined as unconditional happiness, a stable state of heart and mind that emanates from within and is not just a by-product of hormones. The components of joy are contentment, service to others, peace and harmony and wishing well for all. It is devoid of the selfish element that is present in happiness.

In the words of American author and recipient of the Presidential Medal of Freedom, Adela Rogers St. Johns, 'Joy seems to me a step beyond happiness—happiness is a sort of atmosphere you can live in sometimes when you're lucky. Joy is a light that fills you with hope and faith and love.'[5] St. Johns recognized that joy has the flavour of spirituality while happiness has the flavour of material success.

As I see it, joy attracts grace. A joyful heart is a heart that *invites* grace to enter. Grace is an awe-inspiring feeling. When grace befalls a person, suffering is mitigated and gratitude and generosity arise. We are responsible for fostering gratitude within ourselves and in our relationships. Perceiving life with gratitude leads to internal peace and acceptance, even when there is external chaos. Acceptance is the non-judgemental acknowledgment of reality—of life, people and situations—and this acceptance creates space for understanding.

Increase to Decrease

Babuji spoke about 'more and more of less and less'. He was speaking of an increasing (more and more) reduction (less and less) of desires. While we may experience desires, to yield to them without any self-awareness, self-regulation or self-control is detrimental to our happiness and progress. As we discussed, happiness is the settled feeling that the mind gets when something it wants is acquired. It lasts briefly, until a new desire pops up. Joy is the natural state of the heart when we stop trying to gratify our desires from the sources and conditions outside us. Joyousness can become a personality trait, and if it does, it will permanently keep us content and happy.

The journey from happiness to joy is a journey from the mind to the heart, from fulfilment of desire to contentment, from self-centric living to other-centric living, and from satisfaction to fulfilment. Aim to be joyful, and you will become happy. Although, I can't say if the reverse is true.

If Love Is Blind, Why See Hate?

While love is blind with attraction, hate is also blind but with repulsion. If being judgemental is a poison, hate is an intense and more potent poison.

'Laila and Majnun' is a famous tragic love story about the seventh-century Bedouin poet Qays ibn al-Mulawwah and his lover Laila bint Mahdi. The story, as told by the twelfth-century Persian poet Nizami, is a favourite of the Sufis.

A young man named Qais ibn Al-Mulawwah (known as Qays) fell in love with a young lady named Laila—deeply, irrevocably and hopelessly in love. He put his all into wooing Laila; she reciprocated and fell in love with him. Laila expressed her love in a quiet outpouring of feelings, Qays, in lyrics that were elegiac, passionate and obsessive. He shouted of his love in the streets, day and night, to anyone who would listen and to those who could not avoid hearing. He never stopped. Quays became so obsessed with Laila that the locals nicknamed him 'Majnun', meaning madman. When Majnun finally gathered the courage to ask Laila's father for her hand in marriage, her father refused.

With all the passionate, obsessive and ceaseless public declarations of his love, Laila's father deemed Majnun crazy and therefore unsuitable for his daughter. Laila was married off to a wealthy merchant, and a heartbroken Majnun fled the village to wander the wilderness, murmuring love poems to an audience of wild creatures.

Before his descent into madness, Majnun carved lines from one of his poems into rock: 'I pass by this house, Laila's house / And I kiss this wall and that wall / It is not love for the house that has taken my heart / But of the One who dwells in that house.' He signed it Majnun.

Are these words the ravings of a madman? You might think so. Perhaps they are. Or do you see them as an obsessive, not necessarily crazy, expression of a deep love and profound yearning? How do they strike you? Maybe none of these descriptions capture your feelings. Or maybe all of them do. It depends on your perspective.

Was Laila as beautiful as Majnun claimed she was? In his book *Finger Pointing to the Moon*, the famous guru Osho wrote about illusion, projections from within and Laila and Majnun:

A face appears beautiful to you: is that beauty there or are you projecting it? Tomorrow, the same face might appear ugly to you. Maybe it did not appear beautiful to you yesterday. Suddenly, your divine eye has opened up and the face has begun to look beautiful you. To your friends, it still does not look beautiful.

It is said that Laila was not beautiful, it was only to Majnu that she looked beautiful. The whole village was troubled, and people tried to persuade Majnu: 'You are naïve. There are many other more beautiful girls in this village; you are unnecessarily obsessed with Laila.'

Majnu replied, 'If you want to see Laila, you have to have the eyes of Majnu. See with my eyes, only then you will be able to see Laila. If it were possible to borrow Majnu's eyes, then Laila would appear to you as beautiful as she appeared to Majnu.'[1]

When we say, 'Love is blind', we are usually observing a couple's actions and wondering, 'How can these two possibly be in love?' This comment can be seen as an indirect insult, suggesting that we don't see the compatibility, long-term potential or compelling aspects in their relationship. This thought also comes to mind when we think one partner is overlooking the shortcomings of the other.

The saying, 'Beauty is in the eye of the beholder', signals our misunderstanding that attraction based on someone's looks, voice, mannerisms, behaviour or status automatically leads to love. We are saying that attraction can alter our perceptions.

Let us first recognize that love and attraction are subjective experiences. They occur from an individual's point of view, rather than a third person's perspective.

When we observe as a friend or a family member, telling ourselves that 'love is blind' or 'beauty is in the eye of the beholder' can inspire us to accept relationships that we might consider unusual. We acknowledge that emotional connections between people are not always logical or intellectually explainable. We don't perceive them that way. However, let me tell you, we are not seeing the whole picture.

Attraction and Acceptance

Frankly, without the emotional chemistry that overrides intellectual reasoning, no relationship would even begin. No one would fall in love with another person. There would be no room for attraction. Intellect is an analytical tool of the mind, which invariably exposes unappealing aspects, causing love to fade.

Think about our blindness when it comes to children we love. Messy children are adorable, especially to grandparents, who find them equally adorable when they've finished their bath. They appreciate their grandchildren's humour and unconditionally accept them as they are. In contrast, parents focus more on disciplining children to instil proper behaviour, or to stop them from fooling around so they can keep to the schedule. Similarly, when we're in love, we can overlook our partner's traits that we may not like. When acceptance develops, the lack of compatibility becomes complementary, and two partners coexist happily.

Attraction is a natural aspect of our being. It is in our DNA and is a biological necessity for life to progress and thrive. Attraction need not be only physical. It can stem from an appreciation of someone's intelligence, sense of humour, empathy or kindness. We've witnessed instances of students falling in love with their professors due to intellectual attraction or widows and widowers falling in love with a family friend or neighbour through the compassion and companionship they've shared. Love can grow between a captain and their cadets, inspired by the cadets' unwavering sense of duty.

Attraction can occur for assorted reasons, including material goods, power and status the other person has. However, this type of attraction on the basis of external factors often stems from ego or insecurity. On the other hand, attraction based on the mind and intellect is better than the attraction of ego. Let me explain.

When you find yourself drawn to someone based on biological chemistry, the initial attraction is often based on infatuation, fantasies and daydreams. However, as you spend more time together, a deeper emotional and intellectual understanding can develop. This kind of attraction has the potential to grow into mature love.

Through continued association and friendship, a relationship matures and solidifies. The bond between two people is sustained by mutual respect, support and caring. Such a relationship can thrive over the long term, with the couple eagerly anticipating and celebrating the silver, golden and diamond anniversaries that mark their years of togetherness.

The attraction to ideas is triggered by our intellectual consciousness, and attraction to people by our emotional consciousness. However, when we find ourselves attracted to success, fame and power, it's the ego component of our consciousness that takes the lead. It indulges in fantasies of the fame and possessions we could have by marrying a wealthy individual. This attraction is driven by our identity. 'Ego is the part [of our] consciousness that gives us a sense of identity: the I, me, mine and ours'.[2] If unchecked, the ego tends to dominate our choices.

All our attractions are influenced by the environment and our predispositions. Human motivations are so complex that deciphering them is challenging. Suffice to say, who are we to judge? Passing judgement on others poisons the heart and the mind. The toxic nature of judgement eventually harms us. The dangerous tendency to be judgemental often stems from our upbringing and life experiences, so we must be vigilant and guard against it. Let us cleanse ourselves of this tendency, even refraining from judging ourselves.

By practising mindfulness and Heartfulness meditation, we can learn to observe our thoughts, emotions and feelings without passing judgement. In the Heartfulness meditation practice, especially, we are urged to view them as uninvited guests and simply disregard them. Paying attention to them fuels their presence. This principle can also be applied to thoughts and problems in daily life. When we don't give these thoughts attention, they naturally fade away. The first step towards ignoring negative thoughts is to adopt a non-judgemental attitude when we see our mind stuck in a rut or flitting about like a butterfly. Imagining our thoughts as butterflies makes us feel lighter. This approach helps to maintain lightness in both our mind and our heart.

The real reason love is blind is because it does not judge or harbour prejudice. It is devoid of prejudice, sharply in contrast with hate, which thrives on judgement.

Prejudice and Hate

The notion that any race or religion is better than another lies at the root of the evil of racial discrimination and religious persecution. While it may be difficult to believe, more lives have been lost in religious conflicts than in political wars. How could such cruelty be committed in the name of one's God? Similarly, the caste system persists in Indian society, where superiority is bestowed upon those who consider themselves as Brahmins, irrespective of their economic and educational status.

But what makes hate powerful? That it is grounded in the prejudices we have been harbouring in our hearts. Ideas we feel repulsed by lead us to develop hatred. Prejudice harbours hate and can be expressed anywhere in any setting. While love is blind with attraction, hate is blind with repulsion. If judgement is a poison, hate is its intense and more potent version. Love is what love does. Love begets care and has resulted in so many passionate discoveries. Madam Curie and her professor husband, Pierre, are an example. Their shared love for each other and for their work led to their discovery of radium and polonium, which are essential to radiation therapy.

Hate is similar, but instead of creating, it destroys. It destroys not only others but also the self. Adolf Hitler is a classic example of a person driven by hate and racial superiority. Hitler was responsible for an estimated sixteen million deaths by genocide (and another fifteen million by murder and as casualties of war). Of the groups he targeted for extinction, the greatest number were Jews, whom he instructed his soldiers to kill in the most brutal manner possible.[3] In the end, Hitler died by suicide in his bunker in Berlin. No one knows why for sure.[4] However, the precise reason is not the point. In the end, Hitler's hatred led to his own death. Imagine if he had not felt that hatred. If he had not acted on that hatred. Or if he had felt love for, and showed acts of love towards, all those people, including himself.

The Power of Intention

Acts of love result in heroism and pride, while acts of hate result in shame and guilt. Acts of love initiate a positive cycle of similar acts to benefit humanity, and acts of hate leave behind seeds of hatred for generations to work out. This is the case in many territorial wars that continue for centuries in various parts of the globe. So, history is telling us love is the way to survive and thrive, not hate.[5]

Love and hate exist on a spectrum of emotion. Love stands for attraction, and hate stands for repulsion. Intensity plays a crucial role in activating this emotion and the emotion becomes a passion. On this emotional spectrum, hate and anger are on one end and love and compassion are on the other. When love and hate become excessive, they blind us and can lead to disastrous outcomes in life.

Passion of love and anger are fundamental emotions in life. They drive our attractions and repulsions. Emotions also energize our intentions and prejudices. The purity of our intentions forms the bedrock of our life's outcomes. Since predispositions strongly affect our intentions, through introspection, contemplation and meditative practices such as those Heartfulness offers, we can purify our intentions and reset our predispositions. Over time, our intentions become naturally and instinctively positive.

To overcome prejudice, it is essential to develop generosity of the heart. This generosity extends beyond giving money and material possessions, time and space; it also encompasses communication and understanding. When we avoid prejudice and approach others with genuine, pure intentions, we create deeper, more meaningful connections. These connections allow love to grow and thrive with the same intensity that hatred draws on to cause harm. In other words, love, when nurtured without bias, can inspire us to achieve great and beautiful things, just as hate, when unchecked, can lead to destruction.

So why see hate?

Letting Go, Not Giving Up

Contrary to letting go, giving up means allowing our fears and internal struggles to limit our potential by disrupting our activities.

Would it surprise you to learn that letting go and giving up are opposite approaches when it comes to personal evolution? What they stand for psychologically, and their relevance to our growth, is entirely different.

Letting go of our mental attachment is critical when it comes to tasks, projects and people. It allows us to free ourselves from things that do not serve us any more. By clearing our minds of these attachments, we can release unwanted emotions more easily. When we are free from emotional stress, we have the space and strength to elevate our responsiveness and emotional sensitivity.

Ending a toxic relationship, resigning from an unrewarding job, or removing ourselves from a project won't necessarily end our attachment if we fail to let go of the underlying cause. It may be an unhealthy emotional dependence, such as seeking love in a misguided relationship. It could be a negative work environment. Or a project that doesn't align with our beliefs. If we leave such a job, resign from such a project or end such a relationship but harbour anger and bitterness, have we truly let go? It is essential to let go of the anger and the bitterness associated with the job or the person to feel truly liberated, increase well-being and move forward in life.

The Difference between Letting Go and Giving Up

Sometimes, even good things need to be released. For example, clinging to the nostalgia of old, cherished friendships hold us back in the past. While these friendships may have added value and richness to our lives, not every friend is meant to last forever. We can learn from the people who come into our lives, often not until they leave or we disconnect from them. There's no point in fearing losing people or certain aspects of life because no matter what happens, we gain valuable perspectives. These insights help us pave paths towards discovering our true selves. Letting go lets us breathe easier and stay fully present for what's happening in each moment.

Let us examine how letting go shows humility and flexibility, leading to freedom and strength. In contrast, being stubborn and inflexible limits us. The need to always be right and recognized as such keeps us trapped in our ego and ignorance. And where is the freedom in that? When we embrace humility and acceptance, we can let go. These qualities enable us to approach problem-solving with flexibility, focusing on goals and adjusting our methods to achieve them. This is true freedom, flexibility and purpose. To embrace our potential for growth and carry out our aspirations one step at a time, we must release our ego-driven need to be right.

Contrary to letting go, giving up means allowing our fears and internal struggles to limit our potential by disrupting our actions. If an athlete gives up on his training, can they still dream of winning an Olympic gold medal? No, they cannot. And what if Madame Curie had given up on refining pitchblende before discovering the radium within it? If the world-renowned author J.K. Rowling had given up on getting her first book published after receiving rejections from twelve publishing houses, the world would have missed a wonderful series of books, movies and plays for children (and adults). Giving up means surrendering to fear and weakness, losing focus and ultimately failing.

Staying True to Personal Values

Not giving up means keeping the focus, clarity and determination to eventually reach the pinnacle of our aspirations through personal transformation. However, our progress demands that we let go of our preoccupation and, perhaps, even the anxiety about the outcomes. Instead, we concentrate on the means to achieve our goals and stay the course. It's a delicate balance between tenacity and openness to possibilities. Strength of conviction, clear thinking and discernment are tools that can guide us on this journey.

As I was pondering how to act with purpose while being emotionally centred, I wondered about the role of an individual's personal value system. It seems to me that our values lend wisdom in helping us discern the difference between unhealthy attachment and caring for what is good. And where do our values come from?

Our upbringing—influenced by parents, teachers and other caregivers—instils values in us. Our friends (especially during adolescence) also influence us. As we live and learn, we refine and choose or reject those values. Honesty, integrity, kindness, compassion, flexibility, determination, will power and trust, experienced in varying degrees, shape our beliefs and the adults we become.

Ultimately, it is our absolute responsibility to develop our own set of values. This development occurs through self-reflection and regular practice of structured contemplation or meditation, which train our hearts and minds. We must consistently check our progress and hold ourselves accountable for aligning with our intentions. It is important to find ways to reinvigorate our commitment to change and self-improvement. Not giving up means staying true to our aspirations and ideals, and making necessary adjustments along the way by letting go of unproductive or unhelpful elements.

All this is quite easy to write, and may even sound a tad sanctimonious, but the important thing is to remember to ask ourselves, 'What is the life I want to live?' Perhaps the answer is, 'I want a happy life with comfort and meaningful relationships.' If so, can you imagine achieving such happiness with lousy values?

While life may seem difficult and unjust, it is not a valid reason for living without values. Our values play a crucial role in keeping us on course in every aspect of life. Where a co-worker may advance by manipulating and politicking, tempting us to follow those practices, our inner value system, deeply ingrained in our consciousness, must prevent us from engaging in demeaning behaviours like flattery. Over time, we become proud of sticking to our values rather than compromising them for temporary gains. This leads to increased authenticity, boldness and uniqueness, which are key to lasting success in any enterprise or relationship we engage in.

Although a valueless or value-compromised existence may bring short-term success at times, it cannot bring long-term joy. Living without values is just as detrimental as attachment and may result in giving up. It causes personal and societal disintegration. In fact, some of the world's most pressing problems—such as the current climate crisis and the degradation of the environment and biodiversity—can be attributed to lack of good values within groups of collective decision-makers. Wouldn't you agree?

Letting go of attachments and opening the space within to develop values like humility and kindness is not a weakness; it is an extremely potent source of strength for human beings. It is also a powerful tool for personal transformation. For instance, when you let go of a toxic ex-spouse, not only by ending the relationship but also by dropping your ego-driven desire to be right in long-standing disagreements, it may seem small but holds great significance. The act contributes to the development of a strong value system and creates a soft heart. It shows that you are doing your part to keep the universe in a beautiful state of balance.

I believe that letting go is an essential aspect of embracing growth, self-transformation, joy and the ultimate freedom of our soul. However, please understand that letting go does not mean giving up on meaningful work, love or a partner to grow with. It simply means letting go of what is keeping you from living an authentic life to your fullest potential and ultimate freedom. It does not mean you must release simply for the sake of change, a change that you might believe signals growth. It means releasing all that does not resonate with the essence of who you truly are.

Sufi mystic and poet Jalal ad-Din Muhammad Rumi is often quoted as having written, 'Yesterday I was clever, so I wanted to change the world. Today I am wise, so I am changing myself.' These words reflect the journey of authenticity, acknowledging personal growth and the understanding that true transformation begins within. His words encourage an openness to change and self-evolution as integral parts of staying true to one's essence.

The Loneliness Paradox

How we use our alone time largely determines how social we can be. If you learn how to be alone, you will never be lonely.

Imagine yourself alone on top of a mountain, sipping a cup of hot tea, enjoying the cool weather and feeling pleasantly tired. You're all alone and enjoying your own being. You don't feel lonely. There is a difference between being alone and feeling lonely. It is healthy to experience time alone. It can increase the intensity of the connection with yourself more than when you are with others, and when you deepen your connection with the self, you can then deepen your relationship with others. On the other hand, 'loneliness is a painful sense of isolation, a lack of belongingness and an absence of social contact. It refers to a discrepancy between social needs and their availability in the environment'.[1]

Although we are more digitally connected than ever before, we have never been lonelier. During the last few decades loneliness in the developed world has steadily increased.[2] In 2023, loneliness reached the point that the World Health Organization declared it 'a pressing health threat' and appointed a commission to strengthen social connection as a global priority.[3] The mortality impact of being socially disconnected is similar to that caused by smoking up to fifteen cigarettes a day and even greater than those associated with obesity and physical inactivity.[4] Non-digitally, we may be surrounded by other people but for some reason, we lack an emotional and intellectual connection with them. As a result, we don't find meaning in such relationships and we feel out of place.

We all have our moods, and sometimes we don't want to be with our friends or go out and make new ones. There is nothing wrong with that. But when these occasions repeat, they can result in our building permanent walls around us. These walls keep others from approaching us and keep us from reaching out to others. We then have a problem, and it could very well be that of loneliness. When we are lonely, we become uncomfortable opening up to others, even if they are familiar to us.

Psychologically speaking, loneliness has many faces and many reasons. One is if someone has, let us say, an inferiority complex, so that even though they are surrounded by loved ones, they have denied this connection. 'No one belongs to me' might sum up how they feel. Another reason for loneliness is when someone feels they don't need anyone: 'I do not need to associate myself with those people or that organization. I do not want any part of them.' The reason they are lonely is because of themselves. They have such an inflated ego, but if you look deeper, you realize that that person is lonely. And the only reason the person is lonely is because of arrogance.

Both these scenarios require treatment. And the treatment is love. Only love.

The Importance of Family

We humans are social beings. In social psychology, the need to belong is an intrinsic motivation to affiliate with others and be socially accepted. Being socially acceptable is one of our drives. Usually, this love is available in our families and homes. Unfortunately, we don't have the support of local family members people once had. Families are smaller. Between 1960 and 2021, the global birth rate decreased. The number of children per family has dropped from 4.7 to 2.3.[5] Not only are there fewer children per family, but there are also fewer aunts, uncles and cousins. And existing family members are often scattered to other states, provinces and countries.

When I was born, in 1956, in the village of Kalla in Gujarat, families were larger. Our immediate family consisted of my mother, father, grandmother, four siblings and me. Our family expanded then to include the entire village of fifty families. We felt a sense of belonging in the community. We felt safe and loved, which built our confidence and our sense of self.

The institution of family is essential to our well-being; however, a family need not be a traditional one. A family can be two brothers living together. It might be a single parent raising us or a grandparent living with us. It can be a group of dear friends or in whatever manner we experience love. Giving and receiving love is important to mitigate this loneliness. When we have a group of people—at work, at our place of worship or within the community—who can provide love, support and a safe space for us to live and explore life freely without fear of needing to impress others, we can overcome loneliness.

This epidemic of loneliness creates huge problems for families, relationships, communities and nations. How do we get out of this situation? How do we find that sense of community? How do we feel the sense of love and security that a family, in any sense of the word, can provide? First, we need to recognize the serious problem loneliness presents. We then need to accept the situation. And finally, we need to seek help to change. That help is from our loved ones. They are our tools. We need to rely on our loved ones to help us overcome the sense of loneliness, disconnection, resentment and isolation.

As human beings, our well-being depends on our connection with ourselves and those who resonate with us. Connecting emotionally, intellectually and spiritually with ourselves is critical. Exhibiting self-love, self-compassion and self-forgiveness, making positive affirmations and doing things that give us a sense of accomplishment are all critical to a good relationship. In turn, a strong connection with ourselves will help us better connect with others over time. We can remain connected within, even when we connect with others.

Many times, when I would go to birthday parties for my friends and their children, I found myself alone when, for example, I was unfamiliar with the topic of discussion and had nothing to contribute. During those times, I was honest with the others, telling them, 'I am here to listen and don't have much to contribute.' I showed interest in the conversation so that I might learn. If you find yourself in that position, you might make a similar comment. On the other hand, if the subject of discussion is not of interest to me, I remain silent but connected within. If you do the same and someone notices your silence, they may ask what you're thinking about. But no one feels uncomfortable or out of place. Such is the power of being internally connected when external circumstances are not of interest to you.

Let us try to develop a deep inner connection. By developing a deep emotional and intellectual connection within us, we can incrementally extend that connection externally. We can extend it to nature, to pets and then to fellow humans.

Building and Strengthening Connections

I recommend a four-step process to create a deep connection within yourself and with others.

Step 1: Connect with yourself emotionally and intellectually

Connecting with the self needs to be done in such a manner that we connect ourselves to something higher, nobler and more loving. We can start with a simple sentiment of wonder and acceptance—that life is mystical and can be beautiful, and how magnificent it is that we can breathe, think and move around. The question of what brings us into this existence ought to awaken our curiosity and fill us with awe for our own being.

In Heartfulness, we suggest that you spend your alone time breathing and making positive affirmations. We suggest incorporating a daily routine to make that inner connection stronger and more positive. I also recommend that people practise silent meditation with the thought that *they are a part of this great universe and are connected to it. I am open to experiencing the beauty of nature, and that's supporting my existence. I am open to friendship, love and care—to giving as well as receiving.* If you were to sincerely practise this silent meditation, within a few weeks, you would feel a huge shift in your heart towards connecting with people.

Step 2: Connect with nature

Walking in the park, hugging a tree, letting blades of grass tickle your bare feet, or wandering by the ocean, looking up at blue or cloudy skies or gazing at the stars—all begin to create a different sort of emotional connection with the wonderfully expansive universe. This connection is something extraordinary.

When we truly connect with such grandeur, we become part of that grandeur. This connection awakens a sense of wonder within, and gratitude overwhelms us. We don't have to pay to look at the stars in the sky. We don't have to toil to walk on the grass barefoot. When we hug a tree, we receive only unconditional love. Sit down under a tree and breathe in the cool air. Expand your lungs with all of nature's nourishment. Be grateful for such a world.

We could extend this connection with nature to the connection with the source of it all. We assume that we possess a strong connection to the source of life, wherever and whatever it may be, and that connection is why we are alive. The source of light that lives within our heart enables wondering about, appreciating and nurturing this connection. We can dream about and do so many things: correct mistakes, take a second chance, love again, be happy, generous and successful. All this is possible because we are alive. Let us be grateful for this life and make a stronger and more positive connection to it.

Step 3: Show up and be present

Reach out to the loved ones who are waiting for you to show up and be fully engaged and lively. Choose places and people who will promote your well-being. These people could include your mother, father, sister, brother, friend or co-workers. Start connecting on special days, such as birthdays, anniversaries or any event that deserves to be celebrated. This positive reaching out opens up a new chapter in making emotional connections with others. Allow others to know the steps you have taken to become well. Offer to help them out if they ever need you. As you show up for your life, you will also become more engaged and happier.

Step 4: Choose your connections

The next step is to choose the company you want to keep in terms of friends and a partner. This is extremely critical and can be the final success factor. We should orient ourselves towards friends who are equally positive about life and have healthy interests and hobbies. These interests and hobbies can focus on fun, as can the friends who engage in them. There's nothing wrong with that. But those who are intellectually mature and non-judgemental by nature are essential for our mental health. They, in general, feel secure and safe about who they are and what they have. It's important to be with people who feel safe and offer a safe environment to others.

* * *

These four steps are no substitute for quality alone time with yourself—time spent in meditation, relaxation and building your spiritual qualities such as contentment, calmness, compassion and courage. Spending time alone and in these activities will lead to clarity, confidence, gratitude, generosity, engagement and true connection. The quality of our inner connection determines the ease with which we relate to others and adapt to various situations and circumstances we face in our lives.

Thinking and Remembering

Neither light by itself nor the object by itself is visible. It is only when the two make contact that the object is revealed. Similarly, when consciousness shines on an idea or an object, a seed of thought reflecting it is born in our mind.

Thinking is the root cause of a lot of things in our lives. While we manifest our ideas and aspirations through action, it is thought that always precedes action.

A thought is an event or an experience. Thinking, however, is a process. When we repeatedly think about certain thoughts over time, they make a permanent impression on us and become personality traits. Many times, we start off with a seed of a thought and then expand on it, either consciously or unconsciously, and it provides fodder for future thinking and actions. There are studies showing that we have between 50,000 and 80,000 thoughts per day and 95 per cent of these are repeated.[1]

To be clear, we know individual thoughts are different from sustained *thinking*. However, thoughts are like seeds that trigger a process of growth in thinking. It is a growth of mental activity. Like different types of seeds or bulbs will produce a variety of plants, shrubs and trees that appear in gardens and wild forests—some edible, some poisonous, some providing shade to people, some serving as an abode for snakes and scorpions—our thoughts also bear fruits. It is a fact that our actions and the consequences of such actions are the fruits of our thoughts and thinking. Those consequences are varied, some good, likeable, positive, productive and others bad, disliked, unproductive and so on. This clear relationship between thoughts, actions and their consequences should make us quite interested in exploring the quality of the thoughts we have.

Though about 95 per cent of our thoughts are repetitive, the other 5 per cent contain new ideas. This newness provides us with the opportunity to change the past pattern of our existence and create a new trajectory in life. Given that this 5 per cent is offered to us daily, it is possible to use new thoughts to chart a new course in life starting on any given day, no matter where we are. There is always hope of improvement. We have the power to create a new destiny instead of adhering to a predetermined future that was formed due to the bundle of impressions that were imprinted on our psyches in the past.

Variations on this theme can be found in the Dhammapada, one of the best-known texts in the Pali Buddhist canon. The following motivational piece, similar to more modern versions, is attributed to Bishop Beckwith:

Plant a thought and reap a word;
plant a word and reap an action;
plant an action and reap a habit.
plant a habit and reap a character;
plant a character and reap a destiny. [2]

If a single, tiny thought can lead to a full destiny, then evidently having a repository of right thoughts and correct thinking to dip into is critical.

Right Thoughts

Rather than ascribe rightness and correctness to matters of cultural morality, let's assign these terms to qualities of thought that lead to our desired outcomes, whether in our personal or our professional lives. How do we make sure that our thoughts are of good quality? Good quality thoughts emanate from a healthy mind. A healthy mind is one which is properly cultivated with the right thinking and correct understanding from a very early age in life. A safe and loving environment orients children's minds to be healthy and help generate good quality thoughts as they grow up.

The *Mind* is a metaphysical faculty that works in a tangible manner. No one disputes the existence of the mind or the role it plays in our lives. In the Heartfulness tradition, our understanding of the mind is that it is non-local and partakes in the consciousness that exists non-locally. In other words, a universal consciousness. But no one can say for sure where the mind resides, what it consists of, or what its workings are. Research regarding this is ongoing. What we can say for sure is that the mind is the instrument we use for thinking. No one has come up with any other idea of what a thinking instrument is. Many say think with your heart, some say think with your head—these are references made to emotional and logical ways of thinking about a situation.

Thinking is also related to the brain. When someone's brain is better developed, it aids them in thinking clearly. We may therefore surmise that the brain is a tool of the mind.

What is *thinking*? Thinking is a mental act that follows a seed thought. A seed thought is the initial reflection in the mind of an object or an idea. This is similar to light falling on an object and revealing its colour. Neither light nor the object is visible by itself. It is only when the two make contact that the object is revealed.

Similarly, when consciousness shines on an idea or an object, a seed thought reflecting it is born in our mind. Unless we turn away from the object and put our attention elsewhere, this thought continues to multiply in our mind as thinking. Eventually this may lead us to take actions, such as those that would help us to attain the object we've been looking at. In this particular example of an action, thinking is an exercise in the possession of the object.

The phenomenon of our consciousness shedding light on an object is known as *surat* in Punjabi. In the Sikh religion, the name Surat means 'one whose consciousness has awakened.'[3] This conveys the idea that a person embarks upon a self-development journey of spiritual significance after perceiving their inner self as they would of an external object.

Ralph Waldo Emerson, one of the leaders of the American transcendental movement, which was strongly influenced by the English Romantics and the Gita, is credited with having stated, 'You become what you think about all day long.'[4]

This is to say that action gets its force and direction through continuous thought. As action gets underway, it invariably produces results. When we identify ourselves with those results, we get defined by them. Therefore, we become what we think.

Of course, most thoughts are banal. We think, for instance, about scratching our heads or what we want for lunch. But sometimes, we engage in sustained or repeated trains of thought about our futures. What happens when we are mulling over our desires and making plans? Whether we want to be rich and famous or successful in a venture like a sporting competition? The achievement of that success or our failure changes who we think we are. Essentially, our self-definition evolves.

Ultimately, even if our actions bring us success, being happy, finding meaning in our activities and experiencing fulfilment may still be elusive. In the context of successful accomplishment, it is worth mentioning that we only get a feeling of being settled if we become what we want to become. If we do not become what we want to become, restlessness continues to push us to take additional actions to achieve the same or something else.

Correct thinking, which leads to achievement of the goals we are pursuing, is crucial for achieving a state of contentment and mental and emotional peace.

When there is talk about right thinking, obsessive thinking, not thinking, unthinking and wrong thinking and so on, it is an acknowledgment that the quality and quantity of thinking matter. This idea of *quality* and *quantity* brings to our awareness the need for regulating our thinking—both the process and its orientation. Quality depends upon the purity of our intentions and the nobility of our thoughts.

Earlier, you read that when our consciousness sheds light on a desire or an idea, this thought becomes a seed for the mind to expand its thinking on. Combine these seed thoughts with our subconscious desires, ambitions, inspirations and the knowledge we get from our daily interaction with the world and it produces a variety of thought processes and outcomes.

Remembrance: Dissolving Time and Space

Remembering is a mental activity that is similar to thinking. The big distinction is that remembering tends to be a lot more deliberate and conscious. And what do we try to remember? The things we forgot. What we forget is nothing new, it is something we have seen, experienced and felt, but it is not at the forefront of our thinking. Remembering, like thinking, results in action, but it is of a different kind. That which follows remembrance is a deliberate action, taking care of what was forgotten and fulfilling what was to be done. This remembrance also includes those whom we love.

Generally, when we remember a person or a feeling or an experience, it is because we long to be with that thing again—to re-experience it. This represents a sort of love and passion we feel towards the objects of our remembrance. This is especially prominent when a lover has a memory of a beloved. The power of remembrance is such that it evokes, but also fulfils, the craving in the heart of the lover to be with an absent beloved. The person who remembers feels they have a deeper connection to and understanding of the person, place or event they remember. Remembrance brings oneness with what we remember.

Even if thinking eventually culminates in remembrance, it can wreak havoc on our psyche along the way. Thinking and remembering are similar to the psychological processes of internalization and interiorization. You previously read that we become what we think. This becoming (thinking/ internalizing) is still not complete without the being (remembrance/interiorizing).

For example, *becoming* a priest involves learning the sacred texts and making them part of your life. This process is called internalization. On the other hand, in the example of the priest, *being* is experiencing the divine and taking your experience into the world. Christians become good Christians not because of knowing the Bible or reading it daily but when they practise love, compassion and lead honest lives. Muslims become good Muslims when they practise peace and fellowship not just among those who go to the mosque but towards all humanity. Likewise, Hindus become good Hindus only when they embrace all diversity as coming from unity and respect all lives and people. At best, by studying the scriptures we internalize the teachings, but those teachings are still not part of who we are and who we ought to be.

Internalizing (like thinking and becoming) consists of two entities: the internalized (in this case the sacred teachings) and the person who internalizes, while interiorizing, eventually, makes for one. Thinking is like digesting food. Remembrance is like the energy that is absorbed into life itself. Internalizing (like thinking and becoming) is a process that culminates in interiorizing (like remembrance and being).

Thinking is a process that can culminate in remembrance, which in turn culminates in union with the remembered. Pure, undiluted love unites the person who remembers with that which they remember, at which point the act of remembrance ceases.

I remember an interaction a disciple had with his spiritual guru. The guru had been teaching his disciples to practise remembrance of God so they might experience godliness in their daily lives. Since disciples are usually obedient, it takes courage to ask questions. This disciple was brave enough to ask the guru how he himself practised remembrance.

In response, the guru quipped, 'I never forget to remember.' Constant remembrance results in a habit. This habit produces a destiny of oneness with that which is being remembered.

Part 3

Life's Meaning and Purpose

Less Is More

Having less is not about deficiency and deprivation. It is all about having more by shifting our attention to aspects of our existence that hold deeper meaning, like our relationships or a cherished aspiration.

During the Edo period in Japan (1603–1867), the rulers implemented a self-isolation policy known as *sakoku*. Seeded predominantly in Japan's distrust of foreigners, sakoku severely restricted imports and exports. With products manufactured outside the country being prohibited, Japan had to manufacture its own. Yet, the country lacked the materials necessary to make them. The people of the island nation had to figure out how to produce more with less. And they did just that. But how did they do it?

Think about when you've experienced less in your own life. In your home, for example, decluttering and removing unnecessary items (less) provides *more* space and a sense of openness. When your calendar is less populated with commitments, you have more room to do what means the most to you, and you feel a greater sense of ease. Spending less money on items you don't need means having more money in your pocket for the things you do need or for savings.

At that time of sakoku, Edo (now Tokyo) was the largest city in the world. The population was between 1 and 1.25 million people.[1] The city created an early form of a closed-loop economy where everything was shared, repaired, reused or recycled, and no waste was generated.

The inhabitants of Edo showed a mindful use of natural resources. By making full use of the hours of sunlight, they minimized the need for illumination at night. Rainwater was harnessed to create canals and lush gardens.[2] They recycled and reused paper, candle wax, ashes and clothing, and repaired kettles and cooking pots, including fixing holes in the bottom by welding metal patches to them. And the samurai, mostly out of work during this peaceful period, repaired bamboo and rice paper umbrellas.[3] To minimize space and maximize resources, the Japanese people built and lived in row houses. These conscious choices helped the development of thriving markets and the emergence of comfortable urban centres, fostering a sense of well-being for the community. [4] Because of the ingenious designs created by and the efficient lifestyle of its people, the city of Edo flourished, far more than any other region.

Compared to our contemporary linear economic system that generates non-recyclable waste, contributing to carbon emissions, Edo's economic system was remarkably sustainable. Out of necessity, the people of Edo pulled together to create interconnected, sustainable and ingenious solutions to the shortages. The historical legacy of Edo to the people of Japan is not only functional but also aesthetically pleasing. Their innovative approach is a rare example of human ingenuity.

Leading a Simpler Life

Today, there is a call for a change in lifestyle towards minimalism, where people lobby for less. Architect Ludwig Mies van der Rohe, who pared his designs back to all but the essentials, famously used the phrase 'less is more' to describe his aesthetic sense of having every element serve multiple purposes both visually and functionally.[5] The idea is to strip down to the fewest and barest essentials to achieve maximum effect. Although not based in scarcity, minimalism adheres to the same design principle followed during the Edo period when supplies were severely limited, or when food ran low for the princes in the forest.

In the words of the minimalists Joshua Fields Millburn and Ryan Nicodemus, who have helped more than twenty million people create meaningful lives, 'Minimalists don't focus on having less, less, less. We focus on making room for more: more time, more peace, more creativity, more experiences, more contribution, more contentment, more freedom. Clearing the clutter frees up the space. Minimalism is the thing that gets us past the things so we can make room for life's important things—*which* aren't things at *all*.'[6]

Having less is not about deficiency or deprivation. It is all about having more by shifting our attention to aspects of our existence that hold deeper meaning, such as our relationships or cherished dreams. When a couple goes on shopping trips, they can either spend more time together in the experience of shopping or less. For example, one of them might tend to become attracted to all the products, upgrades and deals to the extent that the other spends the majority of their trips siting on a bench outside the store sipping coffee or reading. Imagine both scenarios, which one do you think is more valuable for the relationship?

Minimalism provides a pathway to discover what truly matters and find fulfilment beyond material possessions. 'Less is more' invites us to prioritize the intangible joys and meaningful connections that enrich our existence as we shift our intentions to an internal process of contentment rather than external appearances and possession of things to achieve happiness.

How Do We Comfortably and Convincingly Shift Our Attention to 'Less Is More'?

How do we resolve this paradox in our own lives? The answer lies in the hierarchy of values we cherish. If we cherish people over events and events over things, we begin to focus on quality of relationships and purposes over possession of things. Having less does not mean we shun comfort. It is only to avoid cluttering our spaces and calendars.

External decluttering has a profound impact on our internal state, leading us to internal clarity and creating a lightness of the heart. You may have heard of 12-12-12 decluttering technique, where you find 12 items to throw away, 12 to donate, and 12 to return to where they belong. We have shoes and books all over the house, which we're constantly putting in their proper home. Count up to twelve things in a week you put back in their place. This simple task will also release happy hormones. It's a simple habit, but one that can be repeated easily and with profound benefits.

Use things *and* put them away. This practice reduces the need to constantly search for what we need. Finding things when we need them reduces hurrying and strengthens mental discipline. All of us frequently look for keys, water bottles, wallets and such. Why? Can you relate to this tendency to lose things, constantly searching for what you've lost and trying to keep track of all the stuff in your life? Or maybe you see this behaviour in other people?

The same decluttering practice holds true in the journey of life, as my spiritual guide used to remind me. When we travel light, we can enjoy the journey fully and reduce the risk of losing our possessions or inciting envy of our belongings in others. Fewer possessions mean better relationships. Fewer possessions equal more time for ourselves and others. Less quantity leads to more quality.

In contemplative practices, people from various religions, including those who follow the paths of yoga and meditation, have long aspired to prioritize higher ideals such as universal love, compassion and interconnectedness, placing them ahead of ambitions for wealth, fame, control and power. By pursuing these heart-based aspirations, we contribute to peace, joy and a sense of fulfilment for all.

The Correspondence Paradox

The point of the axiom 'As above, so below' is to make us aware that the dynamics of human existence mirror the movement and action of the entire cosmos.

The tradition of Hermetic philosophy, a school of thought that rose in the Mediterranean region in the second and third centuries BCE, has seven main principles or axioms: mentalism, correspondence, vibration, polarity, rhythm, cause and effect, and gender. It is believed that the universe and potentially all existence is ruled by these seven principles. You may know of the second principle, the principle of correspondence, which is often expressed as 'As above, so below', or in its longer form, 'As below, so above; as above, so below'.[1]

You may have also heard variations of this principle, 'As within, so without' or 'As the universe, so the soul'. All these phrases convey a connection between different aspects of existence. The Hermetics recognized three parallel planes of existence: the physical, the mental and the spiritual. Hermetics believed that correspondence was fundamental to understanding the laws of the universe.

What do these phrases mean for us? How do we understand them and how do they help us learn how the spirit, mind and body correspond?

Duality and Unity

Let us first examine the two sides of this statement. Correspondence acknowledges the duality between the microcosm and the macrocosm, which emphasizes their distinct characteristics and expressions. At the same time, this principle implies unity, suggesting that the two are not inherently separate but interconnected and reflective of each other. It invites us to examine both. Why would we do this? Because humans face limitations when trying to grasp the vastness and complexity of the cosmos, we can analyse what we know to unlock what we don't.

For example, 'As above, so below' suggests that the principles that govern the structure and behaviour of the solar system also govern the structure and behaviour of the atom. And just as the solar system is a part of a larger galaxy and universe, an atom is a part of larger molecules and matter. We can use the maxim to understand how the behaviour and properties of atoms are connected to the behaviour and properties of molecules, and then to the behaviour and properties of the universe.

Here's another example: a conch shell, a hurricane and a spiral galaxy all have the same mathematical ratio to their spiral patterns. We can observe a conch shell to discover the patterns of all three. We can then study a tornado to understand the expression of this pattern and use it to unlock the mystery of a spiral galaxy.

How does this principle help us understand how the body, mind and spirit correspond with each other? The patterns and principles governing the universe are mirrored in the individual human experience. The reverse is also true.

Connecting to Something Greater

The Kybalion is a book claiming to convey the essence of the teachings of Hermes Trismegistus, believed to be a Hellenistic combination of the Egyptian God Toth and the Greek God Hermes. He is also the 'purported author of the Hermetic Corpus, a series of sacred texts that are the basis of Hermeticism'.[2] *The Kybalion*, published in 1908 was authored by William Walker Atkinson and attributed to 'The Three Initiates'. According to *The Kybalion*, the principle of correspondence 'embodies the truth that there is always a correspondence between the laws and phenomena of the various planes of Being and Life'.[3] The idea of a relationship between different aspects of life and being could be considered transcendental.

Let us look at living organisms and circadian rhythms, the daily fluctuation in behaviour and physiology controlled by an internal master clock in almost all living things. Most creatures are diurnal; they wake up with the sunlight and become less active after the sun sets. The exceptions are nocturnal hunters, where the reverse is true. The circadian rhythm in mammals controls the daily rhythms of their physiology and behaviour.

The circadian rhythms in humans also control the biological functions associated with mental and emotional well-being. When we disrupt these rhythms, we negatively influence our overall health. Staying up late disturbs our sleep patterns, which has consequences for our metabolism. It affects the necessary rest and detoxification processes of our body and brain, leaving us feeling fatigued and lacking clarity and freshness in the morning. To be in prime shape to work on the *mental* level, we need to make sure the *physical* is optimal.

Now, what about the feeling of being completely relaxed that comes from being part of something greater than yourself? When gazing at the stars in the night sky or walking along the sand next to the ocean, experience how connected you feel to the vastness of nature. You feel that you are a part of something greater. How does this happen? Our minds expand and become one with the sky and the sea, raising our vibration. When the mind expands, it creates space for itself, and in that space, it finds relaxation. A relaxed mind is a creative mind—wherein innovation flows more freely and one where we can explore and evolve.

The higher the rate of vibration, 'the higher the plane, and the higher the manifestation of Life occupying that plane'.[4] We can take inspiration from the principle of correspondence and consciously cultivate a habit of connecting to something greater and more significant than ourselves. By allowing something greater to make an impact on us, we can influence our physical and mental well-being. The external impacts the internal. And the internal then impacts the external, and so it goes . . . All the time we are raising our own vibration and that of others.

Everything in the universe is energy and vibrates at varying degrees. The greater the capacity for movement, the higher the vibration. On the physical plane, gas vibrates at a greater frequency than rock. The mental plane vibrates at a higher frequency than the physical. Positive feelings vibrate at a higher frequency than negative feelings. If we aim to embody something larger than ourselves—such as kindness, compassion and love—when we interact with others, we begin to emanate higher vibrations of these feelings in our surroundings. Over time, those vibrations positively affect the landscape of our relationships. This is how we start to affect the external (the *without*) aspects of our lives by cultivating kindness, compassion and love *within* our hearts. In turn, we are positively affected by these relationships, and so the external can intensify the internal.

The Cosmic Mind

How do we develop the capacity to deliberately shift our consciousness in such a manner that it shows this correspondence? How can we seek external influences that improve our inner condition and enable us to positively influence the inner condition of others? The following solution is attributed to Hermes Trismegistus:

> Close your eyes and let the mind expand. Let no fear of death or darkness arrest its course. Allow the mind to merge with the Mind. Let it flow out upon the great curve of consciousness. Let it soar on the wings of the great bird of duration, up to the very Circle of Eternity.

The bigger mind, referenced above with a capital M, is the cosmic mind, which possesses the cosmic intelligence that drives the forces of the universe. In *The Divine*

Pymander—a significant, if not the most important, book in the *Corpus Hermeticum*—instead of cosmic mind, the term 'common mind' is used: 'The Mind, O Tat, is the very Essence of God, if yet there be any Essence of God.'[5] Merging our individual minds with this greater mind requires practising contemplative exercises such as those offered by Heartfulness and mindfulness.

Mindfulness is about cultivating non-judgemental awareness. In the Heartfulness tradition, we expand this practice to align ourselves with something greater and grander than we are, just as Hermes suggested. Cultivating non-judgemental awareness is like tilling the soil in a field so that when we plant the right seeds, we can expect a bountiful harvest. Connecting and merging our individual minds to the cosmic mind can be seen as reversing our axiom to say, 'As below, so above.'

Many people have experienced the influence of collective mind without necessarily recognizing it as such. Telepathic experiences are one example. Have you ever experienced your mother, partner or best friend calling you just as you were thinking of them? These events cannot be dismissed as mere coincidences. There is a connection between minds, especially among loved ones. This collective mind is the reason behind finding answers that dawn on us when we least expect them and when we are not thinking hard about the problem. Collective minds can also be misled due to biases, prejudices and propagandas. There comes a negative mass psychosis, like the one which believed and supported Hitler and other dictators in history.

Our minds can also be receptive to impulses from the cosmic mind. The cosmic mind is pure and positive in nature. It is not the sum of our individual thoughts and experiences floating in the atmosphere as vibrations with varying frequency. It consists of the original impulses that accompanied the creation of the universe. It is possible for us to be receptive to the impulses of the cosmic mind only when we maintain a level of purity in our heart and mind. Connection alone does guarantee flow. The channel needs to be open for the flow to happen. As above so below is possible when we develop our consciousness to be open to the cosmic mind or super consciousness. In his book *Cosmic Consciousness: A Study in the Evolution of the Human Mind* (1901), psychiatrist Richard Maurice Bucke defines cosmic consciousness as 'a higher form of consciousness than that possessed by the ordinary man'.[6]

Our minds can be connected to the collective mind or the cosmic mind or both in varying degrees. The more the mind is connected to the cosmic mind, the more spiritual one can be, while the more one is connected to the collective, the more mundane our lives will be.

Numerous philosophical and theological traditions acknowledge a similarity between human beings and the universe. It's a fact that the human body is made of elements—earth, air, fire, water and space—that exist in the universe. Moreover, it's a long-held belief that our minds are connected to the cosmic mind, and that the soul, our spiritual component, is connected to the broader field of the mind. This field is referred to by different names in various spiritual and theological texts as God, Higher Power, Pure Consciousness, the Absolute, Nothingness and more. Regardless of the word used—Allah, Brahman, Sunyata— they all point to this higher field of reality and existence.

Generally, meditation involves closing our eyes to create an inward focus with a relaxed mind. This is how we may experience the without from within. This is how we 'merge the mind with the Mind'. Through meditation, we may feel a deep connection and a sense of belonging to everything that exists. This process brings us incredible peace and expands our mental and emotional stability.

Heartfulness meditation is fully geared towards the evolution of consciousness to the highest level, within the demands of daily life. When we meditate on the heart, the heart and mind work together as one—they form a coherent vibrational field, and this affects every aspect of life. The mind can be fully awake, alert and cognitively functional, while at the same time we feel the profound mystical consciousness of the heart. Our consciousness expands. And so we continue. As above, so below.

The Wish Paradox

The journey from a wish to an aspiration is also a journey from selfishness to selflessness. It is a journey from me to we and from mine to ours. It reflects an expansion of consciousness.

The seed of a wish generally grows into a desire and shapes a destiny. Wishing a good life for yourself and for someone else comes from a more casual place or carries less energy than when the wish becomes a seed of desire. Sometimes, what we wish for can actually interfere with, rather than support us in, achieving our destiny. So, it's important to be cautious about what we wish for. However, some desires, such as wanting to reach our highest potential, can be beneficial and lead to self-realization and contentment.[1]

When wishes are planted, watered and nurtured, they grow into desires. And when we take action to pursue those desires, those actions yield results. The results may be good, bad or even incomplete. So, all our desires manifest through outcomes, and those outcomes have consequences.

When our minds are idle and we let our thoughts wander, we're grazing on our wishes as a cow grazes on grass. By doing so, we pick up a lot of seeds for germination in the future. The danger lies not in individual wishes but in accumulating too many of them. Although these wishes may seem harmless, they can begin to disrupt our life's purpose. Having too many wishes can lead to a loss of focus and clarity, creating instability. This is not what we want to achieve in life.

Wishes Can Be Useful

A wish may not be serious. It's not yet a full-blown desire if it can easily disappear from our minds when we shift our focus to something else, engage in a cleaning meditation (See Part 6, Clean) or even go for a run or to the gym.

However, by recognizing the uselessness of wishes, we can remove them and replace them with meaningful ideals and aspirations. If a wish is inconsequential and based on pleasure, such as wanting to possess something or attending an event, it is better for us to remove that wish or shift our focus to a nobler one. For example, we can engage in discussions that inspire a contribution to finding a cure for cancer. Once we identify such a noble wish, we should nurture it, develop it into an aspiration and fuel that wish with the passion to explore and pursue it.

On a spectrum of thought and feeling, a wish is at the lazier, apathetic end, while an aspiration is at the passionate end. A wish is whimsical, whereas an aspiration is inspired. When we focus on a wish, it serves to distract and drain us. Conversely, when we pursue an aspiration with a focused mind and the persistence of a peaceful heart, it opens greater possibilities. Aspiration involves seeking an ideal, while a wish is more like a temptation. Holding an ideal in our minds helps us transcend obstacles such as financial limitations or lack of a prestigious education. We might say, 'I wish I could pay all my bills more easily' or 'I wish I had a university degree', but that doesn't change our situation. However, if we aspire to earn enough money to easily pay our bills and add to our savings or aspire to earn a university degree, we can plan and take steps to do so. While a wish can bring misery and weaken us, an ideal gives our life meaning, purpose and happiness.

So, a wish, though initially trivial and easily dismissible, can be transformed into a profound aspiration that fuels our actions and shapes our lives. This paradox underscores the transformative power of human consciousness, where something seemingly inconsequential evolves into a significant force for personal and communal betterment.

Transforming a Wish to an Aspiration

The transformation from wish to aspiration is also one from selfishness to selflessness—from me to we and from mine to ours. This journey reflects an expansion of consciousness and humanity within us. We grow from caring about our personal needs to caring for those who are immediately around us and gradually extend our care to encompass others around the globe. Perhaps, it is natural to be mindful of our own immediate needs and wants first, and then expand our circle of concern to include the well-being of others.

We can give only what we possess, whether it is things, qualities or values. If we are strong, we can help lift others. If we have self-compassion and self-love, we can impart those qualities to others as well. So, it's perfectly fine to travel this spectrum—from a personal wish to a desire for the betterment of others to an aspiration to fulfil the highest selfless ideal of human well-being. The problem arises when a stream of wishes fuels an insatiable 'desire machine'.

On the spectrum of simple wish to lofty aspiration, the highest ideal is to become curious and explore our greatest potential. It is said that such exploration requires us to explore the limitless space of the cosmos. Questions such as 'Where did we come from?', 'Where do we go when we die?', 'What is the origin and source of everything?', 'Why is there suffering?' and 'What is the cure for suffering?' are all meaningful questions for us to contemplate.

When our wishes transform into aspirations, we embark on an exploration of the infinite. Aspirations carry the essence of the infinite. It emanates from the deepest core of our hearts, where love, compassion, empathy, kindness and an innate intelligence of interconnectedness reside. We feel sadness when we see another's sorrow, and we feel pain when we see others hurting. Aspirations such as eradicating childhood poverty, exploring the celestial bodies or seeking answers to profound questions about our own existence and that of the universe, come from the eternal space that lies deep within the heart.

These aspirations are fuelled by an unimaginably vast energy. The expansive nature of aspiration sustains itself and keeps growing. This is why we see people like Mother Teresa, other saints and great teachers dedicating their lives to serving causes greater than themselves. We can also find examples in the history of scientific discoveries and philosophy. Scientists such as Nicola Tesla and philosophers such as Aristotle and Manu, among countless others, embody the aspiration for a better human existence.

Those who aspire to achieving their ultimate potential should start by intensifying their desire for self-transformation, which involves a process of continuous self-improvement. This pursuit will be followed by self-actualization (the drive to realize our full potential) and, finally, self-realization.[2]

In Heartfulness, our ultimate goal is self-mastery. During meditation, we remind ourselves that we have come from a Source that created and sustains the entire universe. We aspire to consciously connect with this source, to experience being part of one that is so magnificent and awe-inspiring. With this understanding, we recognize that our wishes are obstacles to our advancement, so we should replace them with more meaningful life goals such as gaining peace, harmony and wisdom.

Plant these ideals deep within the soil of your hearts and nurture them. By doing so, your lives will gain profound meaning and purpose. Remember, it's important to seek assistance and persevere in this pursuit. Success is closer than you think!

End or Means?

An eye for an eye makes the whole world blind.

People often rely on two seemingly contradictory statements to guide them. I would like to explore two of them in this chapter. The first is 'The end justifies the means', which suggests that the desired outcome justifies any actions taken to achieve it. The second is 'If you take care of the means, the end will take care of itself', implying that focusing on the right methods of achieving something will naturally lead to the desired outcome. How do we reconcile the two perspectives? One way is to recognize that the perspective we apply depends on the context.

Let's consider the example of Robin Hood, an outlaw hero from medieval British folklore who, along with his merry men, fought the corruption, injustices and greed of the ruling class by stealing from them to give to the poor. They were known for righting social injustice and redistributing resources. Were their actions justified? Some might argue that Robin Hood could have explored lawful alternatives to helping the less fortunate. Others might believe that freedom and equity must be achieved at any cost.

Focusing singularly on the goal without considering the proper means of achieving it often leads to a 'come what may' attitude. On the other hand, when we prioritize the means to accomplish the goal, we approach that goal with care and methodical planning, aiming to achieve results while minimizing harm or disruption.

Origins

The statement *'The end justifies the means'* is attributed to the sixteenth-century Italian writer Niccolò Machiavelli. In his novel *The Prince*, Machiavelli advocates for cruelty in some cases, not for its own sake but as means to achieve an end: '. . . love is preserved by the link of obligation which, owing to the baseness of men, is broken at every opportunity for their advantage; but fear preserves you by a dread of punishment which never fails'.[1] Some argue that Machiavelli's advice in *The Prince* aimed at helping rulers maintain order and protect their territories during tumultuous times. Others view his approach to politics as ruthless and amoral.

Mahatma Gandhi is often credited with the statement, 'If one takes care of the means, the end will take care of itself.' I'll talk more about Gandhi and peaceful resistance later in the chapter. Until then, I offer this example of focusing on the means: When we were planning to develop the meditation retreat in Kanha Shanti Vanam, that involved constructing several buildings on 1600 acres of land on the outskirts of Hyderabad city, we considered the need to preserve, nourish and nurture the ecosystem. We took measures to incorporate water bodies, rainwater harvesting systems and create an aesthetically pleasing environment to attract birds, bees and humans from around the globe. During the span of seven years, from 2015 to 2022, this arid region of tropical south India was transformed into an actual rainforest. Meditation in such an ecologically ennobling environment heightens the positive impact on one's inner environment. Therefore, when the means are integrated and aligned with the desired end, they embellish and enhance the outcome.

Questionable Means

Sometimes, achieving a specific goal may require adopting questionable means, especially in situations where the rules of engagement aren't compatible with the desired outcome. In Isaac Asimov's science fiction *Foundation*, the first book in the series, one of the epigrams attributed to Salvor Hardin, the mayor of Terminus, is 'Never let your sense of morals prevent you from doing what is right.'[2] This notable epigram becomes a 'half-mocking, half-serious'[3] motto for some groups of characters in the story, emphasizing the idea that sometimes, in difficult or morally ambiguous situations, one must prioritize what is pragmatically or strategically right rather than being constrained by traditional notions of morality. While these decisions might initially appear immoral when viewed superficially, upon thoughtful consideration, they prove to be the right course of action.

In ancient Indian epics, such as the Ramayana and the Mahabharata, there are many stories where heroes employ questionable means to defeat their enemies. While hiding behind a tree, Prince Rama, the protagonist of the Ramayana, fatally shoots Vali, the king of a monkey army, in the back. Killing someone when they were defenceless or unprepared was against the conventions of war at the time. Given the laws of war, were Prince Rama's means justified? Without the protective armour and earrings given to Rama by Lord Indra, the king of the gods, he had lost his divine protection and powerful edge. Vali had been granted a powerful boon that made him almost invulnerable in battle. But his boon had a limitation. He could only use this power when he faced his opponent directly in combat. To adhere to his duty, Prince Rama did not have a choice. However, his decision has been the cause of a great deal of moral and ethical debate.

In the Mahabharata, trickery is used to overcome an otherwise invincible enemy. Krishna knew that the formidable warrior Drona would lay down his weapons only if he believed his son was dead. Through deceit, Krishna led Drona to believe his son—who was very much alive—had died. Overcome with grief, Drona laid down his weapons and was subsequently killed.

The acts depicted in these classic tales are ethically questionable, even cowardly. Yet they were necessary to succeed in noble causes.

Unknown Outcomes

In more recent history, during World War II, British intelligence broke the German Enigma code and intercepted a message about a planned bombing raid on the city of Coventry on 20 November 1940. However, evacuating the city or taking preventive measures might have tipped off the Germans that their code had been compromised, potentially leading them to change it, which would have made it more challenging for the Allies to decode future messages. In the end, British authorities decided not to evacuate Coventry or take defensive measures, and the city was heavily bombed, resulting in significant loss of life and destruction. Yet cracking the code is said to have ultimately allowed the Allies to defeat the German army by utilizing information about where and when they would strike. This decision has been the subject of debate and moral scrutiny ever since. The Coventry incident exemplifies the difficult moral choices and dilemmas that often arise in times of war and espionage, where decisions may involve weighing immediate human lives against broader strategic and intelligence considerations.

In Plato's *The Republic*, Socrates and other characters discuss the complexities of justice. Socrates argues that justice is not about literal truthfulness or returning what is owed in all circumstances. Instead, justice must also consider the welfare and well-being of others. For instance, returning a weapon to an insane friend would be irresponsible and potentially harmful. Therefore, it would be unjust to do so, despite the obligation to return borrowed items.

Let me share a very poignant real-life incident. I know a youth who was ill and fighting for his life, but his kind doctor did not have the heart to break this news to the mother. Instead, he said, 'Your son is definitely unwell, but your prayers might help him recover.' She really believed in these words and prayed sincerely for his recovery. That boy lives a healthy life now. We may argue that modern medicine and science were at our disposal, and they, rather than belief, saved the boy's life. However, the doctor told me that it was a miracle made possible by the mother's prayers.

Given the outcome, which the doctor had no way of predicting, I think it was appropriate for the doctor to not have categorically stated that the child might die and instead, focused on how his mother could help. On the other hand, it is also the duty of the doctor to inform the caregiver of the accurate status of the patient. As human beings, we tend to become emotional, and many of us would most likely agree that the doctor did the right thing.

The examples we've looked at are all complex and thought-provoking. What would you do when presented with such scenarios in your life? Would you justify the means irrespective of the end, or would you justify the end and resort to any means?

When faced with immense goals, such as national security or the safety and well-being of their family, people often find themselves willing to sacrifice their ethics or resort to illegal means to achieve them. It is instinctive, understandable and, to some extent, acceptable when principles are abandoned for the sake of one's country or for survival. However, when this behaviour extends beyond survival and love of country and involves imposing one's will on others at the expense of their families, cultures or civilizations, the means employed to enforce such an end become questionable. It becomes a complex situation where one person's quest for freedom becomes another person's cause for war. In such circumstances, peaceful coexistence and conflict resolution seem elusive, and the result is only war, death and destruction.

As the leader of India's freedom movement from British rule, from the 1920s until the 1940s, Mahatma Gandhi advocated non-violent methods of resistance—such as peaceful civil disobedience, fasting and the boycotting of foreign-made goods. He is attributed as having written or said, 'An eye for an eye makes the whole world blind.' Although it may have been Louis Fisher, author of *The Life of Mahatma Gandhi*, who authored the quote, which was then mistakenly attributed to Gandhi.[4]

Gandhi reconciled his behaviour with the desired outcome because he believed his cause was just. He wisely recognized the importance of media coverage and ensured that the press went with him wherever he went, to shed light on the movement and give it national and international coverage. Gandhi was aware that the resources of the common people of India were no match for the guns and firepower of the British army. His strategic combination of wisdom, intelligence and a noble cause to gain freedom through non-violent means served as a model for many other leaders around the world seeking liberation from colonial rule for their people. Martin Luther King, Jr., in the United States and Nelson Mandela in South Africa are two notable examples of leaders inspired by Gandhi.

In 1893, Swami Vivekananda, a young monk from India, visited the United States to represent India at the World's Parliament of Religions held in Chicago.[5] In his famous speech, he introduced Hinduism to America and emphasized the need to set lofty goals and to forget about them once they were established, focusing instead on the most effective means to achieve them. This perspective, which preceded India's independence movement by several decades, emphasized embracing lofty goals that would uplift all of humanity if they were accomplished. Vivekananda was a passionate advocate for striving to achieve our aspirations and goals.

What does 'most effective means' imply here? Did he advocate using unscrupulous means? Of course not. However, it is for us to understand the cautions and imbibe the wisdom in these anecdotes, adages and historical examples to make the choices that are best for each situation.

Which Strategy Is Best?

When determining the best course of action, we need to consider all perspectives and possible outcomes. We should research, analyse, prioritize the findings and, most importantly, introspect before we make a decision. Hurrying is antithetical to making the correct decision. Hurrying as a habit is a stress producer and a silent killer.

Ideally, we can pause and reflect on this idea in quiet, just before going to sleep. But in many cases—such as filling a lifeboat from a sinking ship—we don't have that luxury. Either way, a meditative mind can quickly discern what is good, evolutionary and ennobling. When such clarity exists, decisions are made faster, even with less information. We should not use meditation as medication. Over time meditation should help us be preventative rather than prescriptive. We will intuitively know what to say, what to do and will exhibit a better pattern of decision-making.

While all meditative practices can improve decision-making, meditating on the heart offers something more.

It helps you leapfrog to the correct decision without going through all the intermediary steps. As if moving at warp speed, you can look beyond desires, break through biases and immediately tap into the intuitive guidance of the heart.

Meditating on the heart results in a better functioning mind due to an ever-evolving consciousness. A regulated mind can focus better. A purified mind can regulate itself better. So, over time, meditation helps improve purity, clarity and regulation, which facilitates quick and informed decision-making. Meditating on the heart is a bridge that connects consciousness with the Source. When you meditate on the heart, it creates a hyperloop, a guidance system from within, so that decisions can come to you very fast. Initially, you may not feel confident in following these insights, but over time, as you listen to your inner guidance, your trust in that radar will grow.

More Is Less

Trying too many things interferes with putting sufficient effort into a few important things.

In our younger years, and sometimes even now, many of us tended to jump from project to project without completing any of them. We may still see this behaviour in ourselves—no matter our age. When we make New Year's resolutions, we may vow to start a new diet or exercise plan but often struggle to stick to the plan for long. With the noise of information overload in our lives, we may have a difficult time focusing on one thing at a time, resulting in darting from one new, shiny project to another. Or we find ourselves trying to do so much just to keep up with and balance work, family and other obligations that we run out of time and energy to focus on—or even discover—what matters most to us.

Trying to juggle too many things at the same time hinders our ability to devote sufficient effort to important tasks. It also undermines our focus. As discussed in an earlier chapter, the principle of 'less is more' holds true. The reverse is also true and relevant when it comes to our happiness and well-being. In certain aspects of our lives 'more can be less'.

A Tale of Two Disciples

Let me tell you an interesting story from the Puranas, one of the most ancient texts in Indian literature. One day, Lord Krishna decided to meet two of his most devout disciples— one a great king and one a cowherd. He came down to Earth along with Narada, the divine sage. Lord Krishna decided to meet the king first. When Krishna, appearing as the elder Brahmana Yagna Sharma, arrived at the kingdom, the king was busy in an international political meeting, so the guards invited Krishna to wait. Lord Krishna waited patiently. When the king finished his meeting, he came out to meet the Lord. The king was distracted by the outcome of the meeting but nevertheless gave sufficient attention to the Lord and then instructed his servants to take good care of Lord Krishna and left in a hurry to get on with the next tasks to mitigate a critical political struggle. Narada was a bit irritated by this. How can the king not give enough attention to the Lord? What threat of war or possibility of peace could be more important than the Lord? After all, when the Lord is on our side, nothing else can affect us. He would take care of everything, right?

But Krishna was unfazed and partook in the hospitality offered by the king's attendants. Just before leaving, he prayed and granted a boon to the king that he may become an emperor and acquire more and more kingdoms and greater wealth until he was the richest and most powerful ruler in the entire universe.

Krishna then set out to meet his other most devout disciple. When Krishna arrived, the cowherd was just about to rest for the day; however, he was overjoyed and, with much reverence and love, invited Krishna inside his simple hut. He had but a single old cow that gave about half a cup of milk each day. That was the cowherd's only food. That day, he offered the half cup of milk to Krishna. Later, just before Krishna left, he gave a boon to the cowherd: 'May the old cow die soon.' And strangely, the cow died not long after, robbing the cowherd of his only means of sustenance.

Narada was terribly upset. 'Why, oh Krishna? I can't understand you. On the one hand, you rewarded the king, who granted you neither attention nor respect. On the other hand, you destroyed the life of the cowherd, who showed you so much respect and love. You are a mystery to me. And today, I am terribly disappointed in you.'

Krishna merely smiled. After a while, seeing Narada's anguish, he decided to explain the rules of the divine game. 'Dear Narada', he said, 'the only thing between the cowherd and me was his old cow. Now that I have removed the cow, his soul will find a way to reach me. He will spend time in divine pursuits and find his way to reach the spiritual goal of life. As for the king, there were a lot of things between him and me: the desire for more kingdoms, increased wealth and greater power. Unless and until he becomes satiated and feels fulfilled, he will never dedicate sufficient time to divine pursuits. So, I granted him more of everything he desired to accelerate his spiritual journey. A light bulb went off in Narada's head and he understood.

Do you all understand the deeper relevance of this story to this paradox of more is less? The cowherd illustrates the paradox that less is more. He had *less* than the king, which allowed him *more* time to develop a greater closeness to the divine. On the other hand, the king had more obstacles between himself and the divine, giving him less time for, on focus and proximity to the divine. He required even *more* wealth and power until these items became less of a distraction, which removed the obstacles to finding his way to the divine.

Our lives are busy, not only filled with activities, distractions and noise but also social media broadcasting twenty different versions of the same news story online. To make room for what's important to us, we need to clear the path of obstacles and distractions. But when our days are full of what feels like so many immediate needs, such as reports to turn in, meetings to attend, errands to run, kids to drop off and pick up from after-school activities—all needing to be done now or sooner, how do we identify the 'more' we need to remove?

Clearing the Path

Have you heard the 'Rocks, Pebbles and Sand' story? A professor was giving a lecture about setting priorities in life. She took a large, empty glass jar and filled it to the rim with rocks. 'Is the jar full?' she asked her students, who agreed that it was. Then she added a small bag of pebbles to the same jar. She shook the jar a bit to help the pebbles settle between the rocks. The jar accommodated the few pebbles easily. Again, she asked the students if the jar was full, and again, they agreed.

After giving the jar another shake, the professor poured in enough sand to fill all the spaces between the pebbles and rocks. Then, with the remaining sand, she filled the jar to the rim. 'Can the jar be considered full?' she asked. Once again, the students said 'yes'. The professor concluded the class by pouring water into the glass jar.

'The jar represents your life,' she explained. 'The rocks represent the most important things in your life, those that hold the most value—family, relationships and your mental and physical well-being. The pebbles stand for less significant, more transient things that you could live without—your house, job, hobbies, projects—that are not critical to your overall well-being and a meaningful life. The sand,' she said, 'symbolizes things that do not matter as much but occupy our daily lives, such as societal conventions, obligations and persuasions.

'The water holds everything together! In many traditions, water symbolizes life itself. The water of life is nourishing, healing and has the capacity for limitless potential, possibilities and spiritual growth. So, it is life that has space for all of it. How we use this water of life and what it represents depends on our priorities.'

Suppose the professor had added the sand to the glass jar first, then the pebbles and finally the rocks. Would there have been enough space for the rocks?

If we're not careful, we can run out of time and energy for doing the truly important things—the rocks of our lives. By focusing too much on less consequential matters, we may miss our chance to pursue our aspirations, ambitions, passion and purpose. When this happens, we need to pour out some of the *sand* and *pebbles* in our jar to make space for what truly matters in life.

Prioritizing is the first step in deciding what can be eliminated from our schedule, either overall or just for an afternoon, especially if we aspire to achieve great things or realize a life that holds deeper meaning for us. What helps us prioritize? One clue is the passion we have for an idea, cause or aspiration. Passion is shaped by our inner calling, which is predominantly aspirational in nature. Mother Teresa, Martin Luther King, Jr., and Madame Curie were all individuals with deep callings. These remarkable individuals were highly motivated and had a profound interest in their pursuits. They refused to let society's ideas of success, failure, acceptance or rejection define them or limit the scope of their vision.

Mother Teresa revealed to her biographers that she experienced a call from God at the young age of twelve to aid the poor of Calcutta. That calling defined the rest of her life.[1] Martin Luther King, Jr., phrased his call to the ministry as gradual, an inner urge. 'This urge expressed itself in a desire to serve God and humanity, and the feeling that my talent and my commitment could best be expressed through the ministry.'[2] Marie Curie became a scientist in an age when societal norms held women back. She not only made groundbreaking contributions in discovering radioactivity but won two Nobel Prizes, one in physics and the other in chemistry.[3]

Staying True to Your Path

Do we all have an inner calling or a calling from God? To find out, engage in self-inquiry. Do you feel a natural excitement when you think of doing something? It may be an idea, a project or helping someone in need. Follow that path. Introspect. See where it leads you. True, you may not aspire to become as charitable as Mother Teresa or an exceptional scientist like Marie Curie, but you can serve your family, community and the world in your own way. You can find happiness, contentment and fulfilment by being true to yourself in how you prioritize. Once you identify what matters to you, you need to fill your glass jar with those important elements before adding the pebbles or sand of your daily routines. Once you have established your priorities, you can attend to the remaining aspects of your daily lives—the pebbles and sand—accordingly. Reflection and resolution can help you find creative solutions to clear the path for what you value most.

If indeed that path leads you to acquire more kingdoms, that is not bad at all. There is nothing wrong with pursuing and achieving our ambitions. On the other hand, if you wish to give all that you have, as the cowherd did, that is all right too. The most important thing is not to judge yourself for choosing more of one thing or less of another. Invariably, nature or life finds a way to get you to live the way that's best for each of you.

Part 4

Wisdom and Philosophical Concepts

Living to Die, Dying to Live

Perhaps it would be more accurate to reframe the adage 'We are born to die' as 'We are born to live'!

Have you thought about your own mortality? Does the idea make you feel uncomfortable? If it does, rest assured, it's perfectly normal to feel uncomfortable with the idea. We all know that we're all going to die someday. We're familiar with the idea that 'We are born to die'. However, there is more to this story. The way we lead our lives—how we conduct ourselves, pursue our passions, fulfil our life's purpose and find meaning—completes the reality of the statement, 'We are born to die'. Or perhaps it would be more accurate if we reframe this adage as 'We are born to live'!

Sometimes, when we hit a rough patch in life, we may find ourselves wondering why we were born or if there's something significant that we're meant to achieve. While none of us has control over the circumstances of our birth, we do have control over how well we live. If we learn to love deeply and genuinely, not only will we be filled with joy but so will those around us. Often, the fear of mortality challenges how fully we live. What if living our lives fully actually lessens or removes that fear?

As children, many of us experience a sense of awe when we encounter nature, and we wonder about the world around us and our place in it. However, as we grow up, our culture and education change us. Our minds become closed, and we become emotionally defensive. We become consumed with the demands associated with our survival, like working and fulfilling our responsibilities to ensure the well-being of our families. In the process, if stress and tension overwhelm us, we may even forget to enjoy the pleasures of life.

The Pursuit of Happiness

We may be rich or poor, loved or unloved, free or oppressed—no matter our life circumstances, we all pursue happiness. It's reassuring to know that seeking happiness is hardwired into our genetic code. In recent decades, extensive research has been conducted on happiness, purpose and meaning in life. Studies suggest that happiness directly impacts longevity and physical health. For example, research indicates that happy people adapt better to change, possess stronger problem-solving skills, maintain a positive outlook about life's outcomes, exhibit greater creativity and demonstrate resilience in the face of adversity. These qualities contribute to a longer and healthier lifespan.[1]

The next logical question arises: What keeps people happy? A long-term study on adult development conducted by Harvard University—one of the world's longest running studies of its kind—has shown that a supportive community, close relationships and meaningful connections have profoundly positive influences on our health and longevity. Primarily, happiness is nurtured by diverse positive relationships. Strong bonds help us experience contentment and improve our intelligence, emotional well-being and spiritual growth. [2]

If our brains are naturally hardwired to seek happiness, why do we often find ourselves gripped by unhappiness at times? It may be because we're looking for happiness in the wrong places, such as money and popularity. It's ironic that while money can take care of our basic needs and improve our standard of living, having money doesn't guarantee an improvement in the overall quality of our lives, especially once we acquire a certain degree of wealth.

Unconditional Happiness

Many of us are fortunate enough to recognize that happiness derived from financial wealth and material possessions has its limitations. Instead, we must prioritize cultivating better relationships with our immediate family, friends and community in the pursuit of happiness. However, even with goodwill and effort, there's no guarantee that we can engineer successful relationships that will contribute to our well-being or that of others. Therefore, we can conclude that the happiness we derive from relationships is also conditional.

My master, Shri Ram Chandra of Shahjahanpur, Babuji, said: 'Happiest is he, who is happy under all circumstances.'[3] His comment emphasizes the enduring nature of happiness that it is *unconditional*, meaning it does not depend on external factors falling into place. The only genuinely lasting happiness is one that exists independent of people coming and going in our lives.

So, which kind of happiness is unconditional? I would say it is the one rooted in self-love. Loving ourselves means accepting ourselves with the flaws and imperfections and recognizing the value of our uniqueness. Building this capacity to love ourselves also makes it possible for us to accept others despite their faults and love them unconditionally, fostering positive and meaningful relationships with them. Releasing our expectations, both of ourselves and others, helps us to develop contentment and improves our tolerance and generosity. If we can make self-love the foundation of our lifestyle, it can truly make our lives worth living. Self-love also leads to self-forgiveness, also enabling us to easily forgive others and accept them without judgement.

'Everyone of us is, in the cosmic perspective, precious,' the astronomer and planetary scientist Carl Sagan said. 'If a human disagrees with you, let him live. In a hundred billion galaxies, you will not find another.'[4] It is all too clear that how we live determines how we feel when we die. If we live happily, we die happily.

Two Sides of the Same Coin

Although there may be two sides, there is only one coin. Wisdom lies in understanding the profound connection between the two sides of any 'coin'. It is through integrating these opposites into our lives that we find a sense of wholeness.

Yin and yang were born from the chaos of the creation of the universe. According to Chinese mythology, yin and yang exist in harmony at the centre of the Earth. During the creation, the union of the yin and yang and the balance achieved allowed for the birth of Pango, the first human, and first gods Nuwa, Fuxi and Shennong.

In Chinese philosophy, the principle of *yin and yang, which dates back to the third century BCE* or earlier, is that all things exist as inseparable and contradictory opposites. The pairs of equal opposites both attract and complement each other. Yin and yang represent the dualistic nature of existence. Yin symbolizes darkness, femininity and passivity, while yang represents light, masculinity and activity. However, within each aspect lies a seed of its opposite. The story of yin and yang illustrates how opposing forces are interdependent and necessary to achieve harmony and balance in the universe. True equilibrium arises from the dynamic interaction and integration of these dual energies.

Pain and pleasure, for example, are interconnected aspects of life like two sides of the same coin. Success and failure also go hand in hand. We tend to group seemingly disparate yet connected concepts, such as activity and rest, satisfaction and resentment, and contentment and displeasure. Naturally, we're inclined to pursue the desirable aspects of these seemingly opposite experiences.

Yet pleasure, success, longevity and praise cannot be experienced without their corresponding opposites. We usually want nothing to do with pain, failure, death or insult, which are an integral part of life's overall experience. And because they're often unexpected, they're even more unsettling. Yet, we can only understand pain and pleasure, success and failure, praise and insult through their contrast. So, it is only logical to expect that they coexist.

Is it inevitable for pain to follow pleasure and failure to follow success? Not at all. Does it happen? Perhaps. Can it happen? Of course.

Let me tell you a story that has been part of Native American tradition for years. A Cherokee elder was teaching his grandson about life by telling him a story about the two wolves that battle within every human being. One wolf represents anger, greed and ego. The other embodies love, compassion and humility. When the grandson asked which wolf wins, the elder replied, 'The one you feed.' This story illustrates the internal struggle between opposing forces within each of us and emphasizes the importance of nurturing positive qualities to achieve inner harmony and balance.

If we become too attached to pleasure, the pleasure we deliberately pursue may be followed by pain. Why does this happen? Pain follows pleasure because we become overly focused on our desires and neglect other important aspects of our lives, such as our relationships with our family and friends and our work. By prioritizing success over health, or victory over friendship, we may eventually lose the very things we value. This path can lead to the loss of health and love, and ultimately result in loneliness.

I appreciate the analogy of yin and yang and two sides of the same coin because they highlight the importance of understanding that which we choose as well as what we avoid. We need to be aware of and cautious about what we actively pursue and what comes to us by chance.

Unity in Duality

To pursue our choices and overcome the challenges we face, we must develop clarity about the existence of duality. This duality encompasses experiences of opposite aspects of the whole: joy and sorrow, gain and loss, connection and disconnection. These pairs are inevitable and inherently linked on the emotional plane. If we become trapped in the ups and downs of this emotional duality, we limit our growth.

Dualities keep us trapped in a cyclical existence of opposites: good and bad, likes and dislikes, attraction and repulsion and that creates a risk of developing deep prejudices against people and cultures. For example, if we focus only on the positive aspects of a particular culture and disregard its negative aspects, we may develop an idealized view that hinders our understanding and acceptance of diverse perspectives. Because they're soft-spoken, we may believe them to be kind, gentle and highly evolved, which might not be the case at all.

By recognizing the pattern of dualities and moderating our excitement and involvement, we can begin to lead a lifestyle characterized by resilience, equanimity and generosity. The benefits of such a lifestyle become clear as we navigate life's challenges with a balanced approach.

Interestingly, opposites are not exclusively about our experiences and perceptions. Opposition is a force that strengthens us, much like the resistance we encounter from gravity when lifting a weight or the friction between our feet and the ground that enables us to move. Without these opposing forces, we cannot progress or maintain even a measure of control. Moving without control is just slipping.

Within our minds and in the interactions between our bodies and the environment, life encompasses a mixture of opposing forces such as friction and movement, victory and defeat, pain and pleasure, friend and foe, like and dislike and so on. Wisdom lies in understanding the profound connection between the two sides of any 'coin', such as a mother's sacrifice for her children and the joy that arises from their well-being. It is through integrating these opposites into our lives that we find a sense of wholeness.

Imagine a coin that rolls along smoothly when it is balanced but falls flat when it lands on either heads or tails. The ability to keep rolling depends on its balance. This analogy holds a valuable lesson for us: we need to moderate extreme tendencies and emotions in our lives, finding a balance that allows us to flow harmoniously.

Two sides of the same coin need not necessarily be opposites; they can be complementary qualities of experience. United States President Dwight D. Eisenhower recognized this when he said, 'Peace and justice are two sides of the same coin.'[1] Mahatma Gandhi echoed the sentiment by stating, 'Love and truth are the faces of the same coin.'[2] The underlying truth of this metaphor is that certain qualities or experiences cannot exist without the other. In fact, they are actually complementary components of a unified whole.

Only if one truly exists, can the other exist easily. For example, in a society where peace prevails, it becomes easier to uphold justice. When love exists, accepting the truth becomes natural. True love engenders genuine understanding.

A Spectrum of Emotions

Let us consider qualities that lie at opposite ends of a spectrum. Unlike a metaphorical coin, which offers only two options, a spectrum implies a range of options. Just as various shades of grey can be perceived between the extremes of black and white, between every pair of extremes lies a middle ground. This becomes clearer when we examine the spectrum of emotions, such as the emotion of passion. At one end, there is rage, while at the other end, we find love. In between, lie emotions like anger, frustration, indifference, silence, attention, attraction, fondness and so on. The extreme ends on a spectrum are vastly different, and we perceive a greater distance between them. At the ends, the middle shades disappear, and disconnected from them, the ends become truly extreme.

When it comes to life experiences, like emotions, the speed at which we transition from one end of the spectrum to the other—for example, from complete agitation to complete calm—depends on our willingness to let go and flow. The more balanced we are, the more we experience life in the different shades of the spectrum rather than at the extremes.

The phrase 'two sides of the same coin' implies unity. Although there may be two sides, there is only one coin. Life follows the same principle. Amidst agitation and calm, there is only one life in which we live these experiences, seamlessly flowing between emotional states.

To approach both pain and pleasure with equanimity and avoid excessive suffering or indulgence, we need to adopt a philosophical outlook. A balanced way of life embraces both sides of the coin. When pain arises and is not resisted, its hold on us weakens. This applies to both the physical and emotional pain that are inevitable in our lives. With acceptance and lack of resistance, we may still experience pain, but we do not suffer from it unduly. Remember, acceptance does not mean inaction.

Similarly, when something gives us pleasure, we should not dwell on it excessively, seeking more and more of the same, as this can lead to gluttony and addiction. Following this path, we risk consuming everything that is valuable in our lives including our wealth, love and relationships. This can cause us a great deal of pain.

Be mindful of your emotions to find balance while pursuing fulfilment. By doing so, you can overcome the contrasting aspects of your experiences and transcend them, creating a more expansive life. You will aspire to achieve the highest ideals of serving others, living in harmony and nurturing an evolved consciousness. Like a coin with its two sides balanced and integrated, your life can roll along smoothly when you balance and integrate the two sides of yin and yang and other pairs of opposites.

Nice People
Finish Last

It is time to redefine the term nice, so we are clear about its rewards. Have you heard the term *intelligent niceness*? It is about being nice to others while taking care of yourself at the same time.

Most of us can remember a time, or times, when we wanted to say *no* to a request because we had neither the time to do what was being asked of us nor the interest in doing so, yet we said *yes* and then ended up feeling stressed and resentful. This scenario is commonplace when we're fulfilling our roles as husbands, wives, mothers, teammates, co-workers and friends.

Even now, in the twenty-first century, I know of women who find themselves taking over most of the cooking, housework and caring for children and elders, all the while struggling to get help from other family members. And according to studies, they often take on these responsibilities in addition to their job. I am also aware of households where men pay all the bills online while their wives watch cooking shows on YouTube. Both partners may despise playing these stereotypical roles, which causes them to resent the situation as well as those who aren't doing their share of the work.

It's no different at the workplace. We often come across colleagues who go above and beyond their responsibilities. They consistently volunteer to stay late to finish an assignment or come in on the weekend. While others may view this dedication as team spirit or being a 'nice guy', it goes beyond that. These individuals find fulfilment in working hard and getting ahead while balancing other priorities.

The Ups and Downs of Being Nice

Often, but not always, people take on extra work because they want to help. However, being nice can often have its downside. Nice people may appear to finish last at times. They may fall prey to others who want to exploit them. But finishing last is always contextual, while being nice is a fundamental aspect of a person's personality. The value of being nice is quite different from the transactional aspect of winning and losing.

Have you heard the term 'intelligent niceness'? The concept emphasizes being nice and taking care of yourself at the same time. Internationally respected psychotherapist Lynn Seiser uses this term to distinguish between the niceness that arises from unconscious, fear-based defence mechanisms and the inherent altruistic nature of an individual. When we can differentiate between (a) giving into our habitual emotional compulsiveness and (b) consciously taking care of others or ourselves, we can be appropriately nice *and* feel like winners—without resentment. [1]

Redefining Nice

It's time to redefine the term 'nice' so we are clear about its true rewards. Historically, building relationships has involved sharing resources and talents. By treating others with kindness, we foster trust and reciprocity. Let's pause for a moment and reflect on this question: When we most need help, whom do we ask? Do we ask people who are qualified and capable? Or do we call upon people we know have our back—people we can rely on? Research shows that when we need help it's often those we've treated well, those we've been respectful and altruistic towards, who come through for us. Being nice matters, and our brains are wired to recognize and appreciate it. As Carl W. Buehner, German–American politician and general authority of the Church of Jesus Christ of Latter-Day Saints, said, 'They may forget what you said, but they will never forget how you made them feel.'[2]

Our treatment of others has a profound impact on how we are perceived over time. When we display disrespect and thoughtlessness towards those around us, our reputation suffers and people distance themselves from us. Although acting out of self-interest or occasionally being mean may yield temporary successes, it may not serve us well in the long run.

Research published in the *British Medical Journal* shows that rudeness lowers performance in certain tasks. For example, medical teams working in uncivil environments struggle with accurate diagnostics and performing medical procedures properly.[3] If this effect extends beyond the medical field, being nice could significantly affect not only your material success, but also the overall quality of your life.

Even so, lately, nicety is getting a bad reputation, while the value of being 'kind' is on the rise. While the two words are often used interchangeably by many, corporations, business consultants, psychologists and many others seem to feel the two are quite different. To these experts, nice typically describes a person who is pleasant or polite to others or putting on a cute act. While kindness comes from deep within, and typically describes someone who performs good acts for others.

This is not to say we don't appreciate those who are nice, but in the workplace, being nice can be seen as a weakness. Kindness runs deeper, leading to deeper connections, stronger teams and greater trust. 'In the "nice" world, you're liked but not necessarily respected. In the "kind" world, you earn the respect and trust of your team because they know you mean what you say.'[4]

To gain clarity, I looked up the two words in the Cambridge and Oxford online dictionaries. In the Oxford dictionary, definitions of kind include 'benevolent', 'friendly', 'warm-hearted', 'considerate of others' and 'sympathetic'.[5] In the Cambridge dictionary, definitions of the word kind include 'generous', 'helpful' and 'thinking of other people's feelings'.[6] Definitions of nice include 'agreeable', 'pleasant', 'satisfactory' (Oxford)[7], 'friendly' and 'polite' (Cambridge).[8] The Cambridge dictionary also defines nice as 'kind'. But for the most part, kind seems to be the more honourable of the two.

Genuine kindness is a valuable leadership trait. When we are kind to others we uplift and inspire them to embrace their own nobility. People bring out their best when they experience genuine kindness, whereas unkindness causes them to withdraw and withhold their best selves and their true potential. The combination of benevolence (acts of generosity and kindness), integrity and ability— but especially benevolence—create the emotional safety necessary for trust to develop in a workplace, community and family.

Embracing heartfelt kindness fosters an atmosphere where creativity, joy and hope flourish, ultimately paving the way for progress. If your primary objective is being the first to achieve something, you may find yourself prioritizing short-term gains above all else. However, if you have long-term goals, the pursuit of 'firstness' may be less significant to you than embodying kindness. While nice people may not always finish first, they are invaluable gifts to humanity and don't truly finish last. Ever!

No Good Deed Goes Unpunished

In this idea of rewards and punishment for good deeds and bad deeds, is there a deeper significance that we are missing as a collective humanity?

No good deed goes unpunished. This statement may sound depressing, going against compassion, empathy and living a good life. It seems like an outcry of someone in the midst of a crisis of self-pity. If we all believed this, it could cause the social fabric of our society to disintegrate. However, the phrase 'No good deed goes unpunished' is a sarcastic mockery of both random and conscious acts of kindness and compassion.

Reward and Punishment

I was curious about the origins and popularity of this saying and wondered what I could learn from them. The earliest reference I found dates back to Walter Map, a Welsh writer who was a courtier serving King Henry II of England in the twelfth century, a period of significant social and religious upheaval. Map's most notable work, *De Nugis Curialium* (*Trifles of Courtiers*), a compilation of satirical anecdotes and trivia was translated from Latin to English in 1923.

In one of the stories in this text, Map describes the actions of a young boy named Eudo, who is deceived and recruited by the devil. Eudo is extremely greedy and selfish and has an inverted sense of morality. Map writes:

> [Eudo] put the worst of men to command the bad, he gave additional authority and power to those who were wickedest in their attacks on the innocent, and promoted over all others those to whom pity was unknown. He spared none of his band who inclined to spare any, left no good deed unpunished, no bad one unrewarded; and when he could find no rival and no rebel on earth, like Capaneus, he challenged opposition from heaven.[1]

Capaneus is a minor character from Greek mythology. He was an arrogant soldier from Thebes who shouted at Zeus, the chief god in the Greek pantheon, who promptly struck him dead with a thunderbolt. On the surface, this is a cautionary tale, but its overall context is that of 'godly' intervention when arrogance is unrelenting. The next literary mention I found of rewards for good deeds comes from Saint Thomas Aquinas, an Italian Catholic priest, theologian and philosopher in the thirteenth century. He says the exact opposite of what Eudo says, in *Summa Theologica* (The Summary of Theology).

> For as punishment is to the evil act, so is reward to a good act. Now no evil deed is unpunished, by God the just judge. Therefore, no good deed is unrewarded, and so every good deed merits some good.[2]

Perspectives on Humanity

When we adopt a cynical mindset, it may seem true to assert that good deeds are punished instead of rewarded might. However, this perspective could be a result of psychological programming. We tend to hold on to the beliefs we've been taught, and changing our minds isn't easy. A review of four studies, each study examining a different group, shows that those who believe that humanity is self-interested tend to cling to this belief, even when presented with evidence of genuine acts of generosity and noble character.[3]

When contemplating the idea of rewards and punishments for good and bad deeds, is there a deeper significance that eludes us as collective humanity?

In today's world, many people advertise their every act of compassion on social media with selfies, seeking validation from the world and asserting self-importance. However, there are fewer individuals who quietly and humbly help those in need, engaging in altruistic acts without seeking attention. For the more unassuming individuals, the notion of rewards and punishments misses the point entirely. Compassion comes naturally to them.

Perhaps, the punishment for those who boast is self-inflicted. They continuously seek validation of their worthiness from strangers, no matter what they do. To truly feel good about what they do, they need to practise self-confidence and appreciate themselves for their acts of kindness without seeking praise or attention.

My hope is that one day, driven by a sense of responsibility and goodwill towards our community and realizing that our destinies are intertwined, we will come together as united and civilized humanity. Being kind to someone is not merely a courtesy, nor is altruism solely for self-indulgence. Kindness goes much deeper. Doing good is an inherent part of our nature, hardwired in our genetic code.

However, it's important to acknowledge that doing good isn't always easy. It is noble, yet it requires patience, willingness and a generous heart to embody nobility in the absence of confirmation or validation. Perhaps, being heartful encompasses being joyful in all circumstances and being open, kind, gentle, positive and generous.

If our attitude is right and our actions flow naturally from within us, there is no punishment for being good to others. We have one life to live, whether we believe in reincarnation or resurrection. If we understand this, then we are by nature happy and compassionate. Let each of us do good without worrying about the attention or reward that may or may not come our way.

I invite you to open your heart and give all that you can give, do all that you can do and enjoy all that you experience.

Ignorance: Bliss or Sin?

If what we do not know won't hurt us, does what we don't know go away? No!

The adage 'Ignorance is bliss' is a bewildering statement when juxtaposed with the idea that 'Ignorance is sin'. Taken from the writings of St Augustine, the saying 'Ignorance is sin' was used out of context, the original statement meant that we sinned from ignorance when we sinned unknowingly: more precisely, to sin from ignorance was to do something which is wrong, believing it to be right.[1]

We recognize that happy people are those who find meaning and purpose in life and execute a plan to achieve the goals that align with the two. In this context, evaluated experience—finding meaning and purpose, evaluating goals that align with that meaning and purpose and laying out a plan to achieve those goals—leads to personal transformation. John Maxwell, a leadership coach, says, 'Experience is not the best teacher; evaluated experience is the best teacher.'[2] Reflective thinking is needed to turn experience into insight. Thus, once we possess such experiential knowledge, we can put it to practical use for the well-being of the self and others.

The paradox between 'ignorance is bliss' and 'ignorance is sin' lies in the value and impact of knowledge. On the one hand, ignorance can be the source of happiness, protecting us from the weight of troubling information. On the other hand, it represents a moral failing, a barrier to understanding and action that can lead to negative outcomes for the individual and others.

How do we navigate the fine line between the peace that comes from not knowing and the responsibility to seek knowledge? When is it appropriate to shield ourselves and others from certain truths for the sake of well-being? And when does such avoidance become detrimental to ethical living and social engagement?

Is Ignorance Bliss?

From around eight weeks of age, an infant can focus on objects, and around twelve weeks, their eyes can follow a point of focus. So if you move the object up, down and side to side, the child's eyes can follow it. Although, they are initially unaware of their surroundings, their curiosity drives them to explore, experience and gain knowledge. As the child grows and learns from their environment, caregivers and education, they become less ignorant. However, as the child transitions into childhood and then adulthood, can we still label them as ignorant if they lack the knowledge they are expected to have?

If what we do not know won't hurt us, does the thing go away? No! It is foolish to say or believe that. Though we may wish to be protected from knowing about the things that will cause us pain, numbing ourselves or avoiding that knowledge is not the answer.

Experiencing hurt, suffering and pain may not be what we actively seek, but we should welcome these feelings as integral parts of our personal growth. Challenges provide us with the necessary motivation to learn and expand our knowledge. We will work hard to move beyond our past suffering, and with time, our superficial understanding gives way to new dimensions of mental awareness, emotional empowerment and cognitive growth. So, we cannot simply discount as or ignore experiences that bring us hurt, pain and suffering, because they serve as catalysts for personal transformation.

The statement 'ignorance is bliss' comes from Thomas Gray's 'Ode on a Distant Prospect at Eton College'. The ending of the poem reads '. . . where ignorance is bliss, Tis folly to be wise.'[3]

The poem evokes a nostalgic feeling of childhood when we were carefree, mischievous and innocent. During our school years, most of us muddled along, learning and growing, fortunate to have the love and affection of our friends, families and communities. All the ups and downs of our school days were forgotten before they could leave a lasting impression on us. Looking back, after going through a few, or a great many, trials of life, we envy the freedom of children, which is akin to being ignorant, playful and therefore blissful. To force unnecessary and premature knowledge on to such young, growing minds would be unwise. So, let children be children and grow naturally into adulthood. This is the essence of the poem.

Or Is Ignorance a Sin?

The idea that 'ignorance is sin' holds more relevance for adults than for children. As adults, we cannot afford to remain ignorant, because that ignorance may lead us astray. So, it is our responsibility to educate ourselves and study subjects that are relevant to our lives.

As we navigate through life, we encounter various roles and responsibilities. We are sons and daughters, siblings, husbands, wives and partners, parents, workers and leaders. Motivated by inspiration from role models, personal ambition, fear and greed, we pursue different goals. On this journey, we also seek meaning, comfort and happiness. To follow the path of right living and reach our highest potential, we need to adopt an integrated approach to life. This means prioritizing personal growth over mere achievements and seeking happiness rather than success.

Now, how do we overcome the ignorance that causes us to miss the mark or commit both small and significant wrongdoings, whether through omission or intentional actions? Before answering this question, we need to recognize that ignorance is not always, or even usually, bliss; it can, in fact, be the root cause of suffering. If the value of ignorance depends on the context, how do we balance our desire for happiness with our obligations to ourselves and our communities?

To attain the knowledge that protects us from making painful and damaging mistakes, we need to engage all our mind's faculties, such as reason and knowledge, and our heart's faculties, such as intuition and feelings. By engaging these faculties, we gain a broader perspective on our experiences and can discern what is truly worthwhile and what should be avoided. They will guide us on our journey to attaining genuine knowledge, overcoming ignorance and experiencing joy rather than suffering.

Practice of yoga and meditation can help us awaken and integrate these faculties. They assist in clearing the past impressions that drive our personalities, establishing noble life goals and aligning all our skills, talents and pursuits. Through these practices, we can obtain genuine knowledge that will lead us to a life of true bliss.

Part 5

Spirituality and Holistic Well-Being

The Science of Spirituality

Since it is very difficult to objectively explain every first-person experience to others, the study of consciousness calls for the experimenter to assess the findings gained from their own experience.

Science focuses on the combination of physical particles (matter) and energy (the force that causes things to move). Both the physical sciences, such as biology, and the behavioural sciences, such as psychology, apply the scientific method to objectively establish facts. So it would make sense that the same scientific method could be extended to studies of the body–mind complex and consciousness. Such an extension challenges the conventional boundary between the physical sciences and the study of non-material aspects, such as consciousness and spirituality. It would result in a fundamental expansion of what is considered the domain of scientific inquiry.

Today, consciousness is considered as fundamental to life as Newton's physics. The study of consciousness in all its facets from quantum entanglement to biogenic connection to our thinking and mental health is just beginning. Yet, does scientific inquiry adequately address non-physical phenomena such as consciousness?

Traditionally, Western scientists have embarked on a path of inquiry, asking questions relating to what the universe is made of and seeking to understand the Earth's relationship with other celestial objects. While thinkers from the Eastern world embarked on the questions of 'Why are we born?' and 'What is our relationship with the rest of creation?' This line of thinking led the conversation on consciousness approximately between 2500 and 5000 years ago, as evidenced in ancient literature such as *The Ashtavakra Gita* and *The Yoga Vasistha*.

The Study of Consciousness

The study of consciousness includes the various mental and emotional states exhibited not only by human beings but also by diverse life forms. Ideally, this would include the study of the consciousness of statues of stone to angels and beyond. There is growing curiosity in academic circles to study crystals in the presence of varied groups of observers with different attitudes. Stones, too, have consciousness, which is on a spectrum different from that of living organisms. For example, stones have no awareness, no cognizance and no discretion, yet they are made from atoms and particles of energy and they emit radiation.[1]

As far as human beings are concerned, if the study of consciousness were to merge with the study of emotional intelligence, which is marked by the existence of empathy and compassion, we would need to be both the researchers and the subjects of the study. Why? Because it is very difficult for people to objectively explain every first-person experience to others, the study of consciousness calls for those conducting the experiment to assess the findings gained from their own experience, which would render the findings invalid according to the scientific method.

Still, Lord Buddha followed this process of being both the experimenter and the subject. Twenty-five hundred years ago, on his path to enlightenment, he conducted experiments on himself to learn the effects of meditation and breathing on mental and physical well-being, on spiritual advancement and to find answers to numerous questions. The conclusions he drew were based on his own experience.

While the Buddha's experiments with meditation would have been considered subjective, over time, the understanding and knowledge he gained became valuable for many people. What was true for him could also be applied to society at large. For you, it will be the same. As you continue to meditate, your perspective expands. That expansion continues and, over time, the conclusions you draw and the knowledge you gain from your many experiences form your conclusion. At first, you are like a young bud, and as you continue and deepen your practice, like a bud, you open and then you blossom.

Spiritual Science

Traditionally, this subjective method is called the science of spirituality. This science deals with self-improvement through the study of the inner self or the psychic self. The study requires introspection, contemplation and other mental exercises. These mental exercises are done from a person's home and must be balanced with good health, which includes yoga. The comprehensive science of yoga includes physical (exercise, nutrition and herbal therapy), mental, emotional, intellectual, behavioural and spiritual practices for the overall well-being of an individual. The purpose of this science is for a person to gain spiritual knowledge and transform to their highest spiritual potential.

Similar to other sciences, the knowledge of spiritual science also evolves. Although with spiritual science, which relies on first-person experience, the duration of the experiment is a lifetime. And unlike the benefits of electricity or fertilizer experienced by so many, the adoption of spiritual practices that have risen from spiritual science and experimentation is limited to a few. The second problem with the science of spirituality is its propensity to promote pseudo-scientists. Because of this, we find a great number of charlatans in spirituality. As the science of spirituality involves the study of consciousness along with emotional intelligence, it deals with tools and techniques to observe and experiment in that realm. This realm consists of all that makes an individual unique— their inner psychology, mental development, family and societal upbringing and so on. In other words, an individual's personality. Now the question is, how do we evolve the personality we're born with into something we aspire to become? In physical sciences, we would set a hypothesis based on an observation and go about proving or disproving it. In the realm of spiritual science, we must set similar hypotheses for ourselves and then start the journey of proving or disproving them.

Spirituality Is Also a Science of Integration

Those who have embarked on such journeys have recommended that we extricate ourselves from the so-called lower tendencies of the mind, which are pleasure-oriented, desire-filled and fear-based. Instead, we must focus on the aspirational common good, and the ultimate potential of experiencing connectedness and centredness. Then, we can say that spirituality can be considered a science of integration.

This science of integration can assimilate the purpose of life with the search and activity of life, the quality of the soul with what the mind should aspire to, and what we expect from others with what we are ourselves becoming. This science integrates rationality with faith, love with discipline, duty with compassion and truth with understanding.

If we look at spirituality through this lens, we can appreciate that it is an inner science that considers multiple variables, and so, it may not be comparable to a mathematical equation. Yes, there are complex equations in the realm of cosmology, astrophysics and social sciences. But as we stand today, the so-called spiritual, or sacred, geometry (an ancient science that explores and explains the energy patterns that create and unify all things) remains a conversation and not a study that is well understood, articulated or followed. However, there is a general cause-and-effect relationship of thought and action, and action and consequence. This is the simple starting point for humans to develop proper behaviour and aspire for a nobler life.

The Science of the Self

Looking at spirituality through the lens of religion is not fair; religions have belief systems and a hierarchical approach, that give the idea of God a persona. We should look at spirituality as the science of the self, in all its complexity, connection and wholesomeness.

There are a growing number of people who define themselves as spiritual but not religious (SBNR). This group of people does not consider their spiritual growth or the evolution of their consciousness to be dependent on organized religion in any way. Pew Research found that 22 per cent of Americans considered themselves to be SBNR because they are spiritual or they consider spirituality very important in their lives, but they neither think of themselves as religious nor say religion is very important in their lives.[2]

Data from the US National Study of Youth and Religion indicates that while they might not be aware of it, the practices and beliefs most embrace are Dharmic.[3] The word 'dharma' comes from Sanskrit, and literally means 'decree or custom'. 'In various religious, philosophical, and cultural traditions originating in India: a distinctive aspect of truth or reality; (also) a spiritual path to be followed by a person or group in fulfilment of the eternal law of the cosmos.'[4]

The evidence shows that spirituality being looked upon as a science is as attractive to today's minds as the physical sciences. This is also largely due to the fact that faith-based religions have disappointed the rational minds who are exploring the powers of the world and human potential beyond the physical sciences.

The field of yoga and meditation is entering universities, businesses and wellness organizations for in-depth scientific research. Its relevance has been seen in creativity, productivity, employee satisfaction, profitability and overall human well-being. In the book *Altered Traits: Science Reveals How Meditation Changes Your Mind, Brain and Body*, authors

Daniel Goleman and Richard J. Davidson, write about three broad categories of meditation—mantra meditation, breathing meditation and devotional meditation. They conclude that while all these categories positively impact emotional intelligence, devotional meditation seems to have the greatest impact.[5]

I encourage you to ignore the antagonistic debate between physicists and priests, where religious scholars try to justify everything that is metaphorical in the scriptures as real, and the scientists do not want to acknowledge the existence of unseen forces and unknown forces that are beyond physics. The physicists and priests are constantly trying to disprove each other. This argument is opposed to the search for spiritual truth. I'm afraid neither will find it. It is left to us individuals to set a goal to be the next best versions of ourselves and set our minds to achieve it. Once we achieve that version, we may advance to the next better version.

Accordingly, we evolve our consciousness day-by-day. This is a worthy goal that allows us to develop in all aspects of life. This is also the *ikigai* (a reason for being) for each of us and would make us proud, happy, healthy and purposeful.[6] In this, we are the experiment and the experimenter, and the result of such experiments as well. I hypothesize that if we set our mind to it, we can become the perfect version of ourselves in this lifetime—happy, intelligent, compassionate and more!

Faith: Belief in the Impossible

Faith is a prelude to finding meaning and purpose in life. It is a form of optimism or hope for help of some kind from an invisible power.

People often say, 'Faith moves mountains.' The biblical reference is more concise. The apostles ask Lord Jesus why their efforts to cast a demon from a young boy have failed. Jesus answers, 'Because you have so little faith. Truly, I tell you, if you have faith as small as a mustard seed, you can say to this mountain, "Move from here to there," and it will move. Nothing will be impossible for you.'[1] Lord Jesus uses the metaphor of a mustard seed—while certainly not the smallest seed in the world, perhaps the smallest seed his listeners were aware of—to illustrate that with just this smallest bit of faith, nothing is impossible, including moving a mountain.

Rationally, of course, moving a mountain seems impossible. None of us has seen a mountain move, except perhaps during an earthquake or a volcanic eruption when tectonic plates cause that movement, but even then, it's the slightest amount. The movement of tectonic plates that grind together to form mountains is so gradual that the shape of the landscape changes over millennia. We know that earthquakes, lava and tectonic plates are real, but we don't know if the emergence of mountains has anything to do with our personal faith. It is a metaphor for the power of faith.

So in addition to a mustard-seed portion of faith, fasting and prayer are mentioned in many versions of the Bible, often cited in some manuscripts as verse 21: 'Howbeit this kind goeth not out but by prayer and fasting,'[2] suggesting that spiritual disciplines can enhance the power of faith.

The Flexible Mind

One of my spiritual teachers defined faith as belief in the impossible. This definition makes sense, although it is not entirely rational. For the logical mind, something impossible cannot, under any conditions, occur. How could a rational person believe in the impossible? One of the paradoxes of life is that it is not all about rational thinking. The curiosity of the flexible mind and the anticipation of something wonderful revealing itself to us as a surprise in the future push us forward.

In one way, science, which is based on discovery, is past-oriented, like the study of history. Each advancement in research builds on past discoveries. However, new discoveries also occur, leading to greater knowledge and innovation that will improve people's lives in the future. For example, the discovery of DNA's structure in the 1950s was built on previous research in genetics and biology, but it also paved the way for groundbreaking advancements such as gene therapy, personalized medicine and CRISPR[3] gene editing technology. These innovations continue to shape the future of healthcare and improve lives. Although science is grounded in logic and evidence, scientists often rely on intuition and instinct to form their hypotheses and make creative connections in their research design. They have the passion and drive to follow their instinctual curiosity.

While developing the theory of relativity, theoretical physicist Albert Einstein imagined himself riding alongside a beam of light. This mental exercise, based more on intuition than experimental evidence, led him to conceive of the idea that time is not absolute and can vary depending on the observer's speed. Alexander Fleming, a Scottish physician and microbiologist, discovered penicillin accidentally when he found that mould had killed bacteria growing in a Petri dish. Instead of throwing out the ruined experiment, he followed his instinct to investigate further. Dr Kamal Ranadive's intuition that viruses could be involved in certain types of cancer—an idea that was treated with scepticism at the time—forged ahead, contributing significantly to the understanding of cancer biology. Through rigorous research, trust in their intuition and drive, these scientists made some of the most significant discoveries in history.

Faith Plus Action

Is it an exercise in faith to propose a hypothesis before a study begins? You could say so. Faith can be a prelude to finding meaning and purpose in life. It is a form of optimism or hope for help of some kind from an invisible power. Psychologist Martin Seligman, director of the Positive

Psychology Center at the University of Pennsylvania, writes, 'Positive Psychology takes seriously the bright hope that if you find yourself stuck in the parking lot of life, with few and only ephemeral pleasures, with minimal gratifications, and without meaning, there is a road out. This road takes you through the countryside of pleasure and gratification, up into the high country of strength and virtue, and finally to the peaks of lasting fulfilment: meaning and purpose.'[4]

There is a danger when faith comes with a set expectation. As we all know, in life, not every desire or expectation is fulfilled. If we are disappointed too many times, our resolve to pursue what is important to us weakens, or worse, it's destroyed. Faith can be antithetical to personal effort if it is not properly understood. Faith alone does not 'move mountains'. But faith, in combination with perseverance and positive action, does improve the probability of our success. What is probable is, by definition, always possible.

Understanding the difference between the kind of faith that begets hope and the kind of faith that begets positive action is the key to self-confidence and higher levels of achievement in our lives. Faith combined with action boosts our happiness and well-being. Taking a positively expectant approach means leading a life of faith that neither shuns rational thinking nor embraces wishful thinking. Faith, in the right context and expressed with proper understanding, strengthens us and is a virtue. However, faith that promotes the expectation of getting something for nothing, while making no effort or contribution, is not.

Perhaps, we should consider faith as the pause between the culmination of our efforts and the blossoming of our results. That moment when we've done all we can do, when we wait to see what happens while at the same time remaining unattached to the results. Faith has an element of patience and acceptance of things beyond our control. The contemplative practices of many traditions are designed to help us cultivate qualities of calm and contentment while remaining aspirational. Faith is the by-product of the lived experience of holding space for the good to unfold after having sown the seeds of such goodness.

Cultures, religions and movements all have stories that highlight the idea that faith supplemented with action can lead to extraordinary outcomes. They teach that faith in a higher power, in oneself or in a righteous cause can empower individuals to face and overcome great challenges.

Many people say they believe in God and consider that enough. But belief alone is very superficial. Meditation is a way of taking the next step, and the next, and so on. When we are new to meditation, we might express this idea in our own way: 'God, I truly don't know if you are there or not. I like to believe that you are there, but if you are there, I'd like to experience your presence'. This is an example of a prayerful heart.

When the *experience* of meditation arises in our hearts, we develop *faith* in that experience, and that faith leads to *trust*, which leads to a certain dependence on the practice. In time, that trust flowers into a state of *surrender*, which might be expressed as 'whatsoever happens because of this practice is always good for me'.

The God Principle

Laws are constants in nature, so they do not 'reward' or 'punish' anyone or anything arbitrarily or otherwise.

In ancient Greece, a wagoner was once driving a heavy load along a very muddy way. At last, he came to a part of the road where the wheels sank halfway into the mire, and the more the horses pulled, the deeper the wheels sank. So the wagoner threw down his whip, and knelt down and prayed to Hercules the Strong.

'O Hercules, help me in this my hour of distress,' he cried.

Hercules appeared to him and said, 'Tut, man, don't sprawl there. Get up and put your shoulder to the wheel. The gods help them that help themselves.'[1]

Aesop's fable of 'Hercules and the Wagoner' shows a departure from traditional Abrahamic (Judaism, Christianity and Islam) religious views of an authoritarian god of reward and punishment. Rather than depicting humanity as being subject to the arbitrary will of a deity, it offers humanity a form of empowerment.

Spinoza's God

Seventeenth-century Dutch philosopher Baruch Spinoza, who is considered a great rationalist and secular theologist, conceived of God not as an individual entity or a creator but as the 'sum of the natural and physical laws of the universe'.[2] Spinoza's view of God is similar to what Buddhism calls the mystic law. To Spinoza, God was the substance of the universe, and in Buddhism, the Dharma (the mystic law of cause and effect) is the life of the universe.

Nobel Prize-winning physicist Albert Einstein was so taken with Spinoza's definition that when Rabbi Herbert Goldstein sent a telegram asking, 'Do you believe in God?' Einstein replied, 'I believe in Spinoza's God, who reveals Himself in the lawful harmony of the world, not in a god who concerns himself with the fate and the doings of mankind.'[3]

God as Natural Phenomenon

It might come as a surprise to you that a self-declared agnostic physicist would accept anybody's point of view on God. But perhaps it makes sense that a scientist studying natural phenomena would embrace the philosopher's neutral view of God, who never argued against the existence of God, but one who challenged doctrinal orthodoxy, particularly on moral issues.[4] If God is nature or God created nature, then God's laws must be synonymous with the natural phenomena we observe in the world, such as the laws of gravity, motion, thermodynamics and so forth.

This perspective implies that the orderly and consistent patterns we observe in the universe, from the smallest particles to the vastness of space, are direct manifestations of divine will or design. So understanding the physical laws of the universe is, in a way, understanding the intentions or the framework established by God.

If God were a natural principle, like one of the laws of physics, as with any other law, couldn't we harness the law of God for our betterment? Humans have been harnessing the forces of nature to improve their lives since early hominids discovered fire for cooking and heating: water pumps, windmills for grinding grain, hydroelectric dams for power, solar panels for energy.

Laws are constants in nature, so they do not 'reward' or 'punish' anyone or anything arbitrarily or otherwise. Speaking metaphorically, however, you might say that physical laws are *kind* to those who abide by them and *unkind* to those who resist them. For example, skydivers rely on the precise application of gravitational and aerodynamic principles to safely navigate their descent. Disregarding these laws? That's not a good idea. When architects design buildings, they meticulously adhere to the laws of physics. By doing so, they ensure their structures can withstand forces like gravity and wind. If they ignore these principles, they risk the structure collapsing.

But it would be absurd to say that gravity—or any other law of nature—is deliberately hindering or helping anyone. Gravity, like all natural laws, functions impartially and universally, applying the same principles to every object regardless of context. It operates independent of our desires or perceptions. To attribute motives such as 'hindering' or 'helping' to these impersonal forces would be to misunderstand their nature. By extension, if we agree with Spinoza that God is nature, then it is evident that God neither rewards nor punishes people.

A wonderful thing about natural laws is that they operate inexorably. We don't need to think about gravity for it to keep us rooted on the planet. Of course, gravity can be bothersome when we are carrying heavy grocery bags. It can tire us out if we are climbing a steep hill. In these instances, it might seem as though the law of gravity is working against us. But there are occasions when gravity seems friendlier and more helpful. For example, gravity makes schussing down a snow-covered hill fun.

Despite gravity's constant presence, its influence parallels lessons from various wisdom traditions on the importance of personal effort. Some versions of Aesop's 'Hercules and the Wagoner' end with Hercules saying, 'Hercules will not help unless you make the effort to help yourself.' A similar sentiment can be found in the Quran: 'Indeed Allah will not change the conditions of a population until they change what is in themselves.'[5] And in the Bhagavad Gita (6.1): 'The Supreme Personality of Godhead said: One who is unattached to the fruits of his work and who works as he is obligated is in the renounced order of life, and he is the true mystic, not he who lights no fire and performs no duty.'[6] The main point in these examples is that if we want God's help, we cannot simply sit around whining, 'Please, God. Help me.' No. We need to stand up and get to work.

Given the scale of nature's activity compared to ours, maybe it is more meaningful to ask what connection exists between God and human beings? The question 'what is God?' has been a subject of debate by philosophers and theologians since time immemorial.

Borrowing Spinoza's definition of God, the evidence indicates that God exists, in a certain manner, as the laws of nature exist. But laws do not have a mind, so perhaps

God has no 'mind' either? It would take a mind to judge our actions as 'good' or 'bad', wouldn't it? If God is a principle and has no mind, once again we conclude that God can neither punish nor reward us.

This perspective offers us freedom from the fear of divine retribution that some religious people teach. It also frees us from the temptation of behaving virtuously solely for the promise of a heavenly reward. Instead, it encourages living a moral and ethical life for its own sake, valuing goodness and right action without the expectation of reward or fear of punishment in an afterlife. This perspective would lead to a more intrinsic motivation for lasting ethical behaviour, focusing on the inherent value of actions rather than external rewards.

There is a growing number of people in the world who consider themselves spiritual but not religious. They are curious about the workings of God but do not subscribe to ideas of divine retribution or reward for the followers of one faith more than others. For them, seeking God in nature is often a religious experience. In this way, the natural world embodies the world of spirit or simply how they feel, perceive and conduct their lives. God does not act upon us but is instead the very fabric of existence that, when understood and respected, empowers us to shape our destiny in harmony with the cosmos.

Whether nature is God from a religious point of view, or not, it has properties that are beneficial to us. The fact that such an intricate and diverse system exists on our planet, and runs so harmoniously, is awe-inspiring and expresses an intelligence beyond our understanding. Nature is able to rebalance itself despite the imbalance caused by our activities. The rebalance might come about in the form of a change of seasons or climate change. The broader idea is that by understanding the laws of nature, which includes the nature of all life forms, we can coexist, thrive and evolve our knowledge and intelligence. The fact that we are sustained by nature may be a sign of God's invisible presence, just like the swaying movement of tree branches is a sign of the presence of wind.

The Nothingness Paradox

What exactly is peace? We may not be able to define it without emphasizing how we feel when we lack peace.

If I told you that your goal must be nothingness and nothing short of it, would you be inclined to read or listen to me further? It might sound nonsensical and unrelatable. However, it is a spiritual truth that from nothingness come all things. 'Nothingness' is not nothing. It is unalloyed, pure potential. What manifests from the pure potential is the intention. However, the spiritual journey takes you through peace and bliss to nothingness. Immense happiness must result in joy. Immense joy should result in peace, which in turn should result in bliss. Immense bliss should yield to nothingness.

In Hinduism, the prayer for peace is a prayer for oneself, all humanity and the entire universe. Buddhists also pray for peace in their body, mind and speech. But what exactly is peace? To understand peace, we must consider how we feel when we lack it. Lack of peace brings restlessness, unhappiness, discontent, conflicts, confusion, fear, heartbreak and relationship problems. By contrast, when we experience peace, none of these negative qualities are present.

Peace is often understood as a state of tranquillity or serenity, free from disturbance or conflict. It is characterized by a calm, steady state of being that is not easily shaken by external circumstances. Peace is about harmony within oneself and with the external world, suggesting a balanced and grounded state of existence, one that is often seen as sustainable and enduring—a foundational state that allows for the presence of other positive experiences.

The Many Faces of 'Peace'

Everyone desires to live a stress-free life and enjoy it without obstacles. Many of us chase after endless pleasures (which cause a momentary sense of satisfaction or enjoyment), instant gratification and ego satisfaction, thinking that these will bring us peace. Across the world, a significant portion of the population seeks to escape poverty and injustice. For them, peace means having their basic needs met.

Others have different ideas about what constitutes peace. Some people mistake pleasure for happiness and equate success with acquiring material possessions. They pursue their ambitions and crave—and attract—attention without considering the consequences. They are looking for happiness in the wrong places. It seems that their pursuit of happiness has been overshadowed by the pursuit of success and power.

Even those who achieve success and power may experience only fleeting moments of peace if they still carry restlessness in their hearts and minds. True peace can only be obtained when this restlessness subsides. If they can eliminate the causes of their restlessness, they may find a more lasting state of peace. One way to reduce restlessness is to focus on higher aspirations or ideals and meditate consistently, which also improves focus over time.

Peace is an emotional state characterized by a feeling of calm and a quiet mind. For most of us, this peace is situational and temporary. Therefore, we need to work on cultivating peace every day, even while navigating our daily material world.

How Can We Achieve Peace?

Peace becomes possible when we cultivate contentment. And how do we attain contentment? By controlling our desires and being grateful for what we already have.

Controlling desires can be challenging because desires, as extensions of wishes, are numerous by nature and may multiply and spread uncontrollably. Keeping them in check is a lifelong mission. However, the approach I suggested to check restlessness (focusing on higher aspirations and goals along with a meditation practice) can also help manage desires.

When I was a teenager, one of my teachers drew a line on the blackboard and asked, 'How would you make this line smaller without erasing it?' After a few moments of silence, he said as he drew, 'by drawing a bigger line next to it.' He was teaching us how to gain perspective when we have numerous desires in life. The solution lies in having a noble and lofty purpose in life that inspires us to achieve.

In this context, it's important to understand the difference between ambition and aspiration. Ambition drives us to pursue success and accumulate possessions, achievements and recognition, while aspiration motivates us to seek solutions to the larger problems facing humanity. Aspiration helps keep desires in check since they are always self-centred. Someone driven by ambition finds no peace, while someone who aspires to solve larger problems, feels peaceful and experiences benefits beyond peace. Someone driven by aspiration undergoes a process of self-transformation and actively pursues excellence in everything they do. The lesson is that while aiming for perfection, even stumbling upon excellence is a meaningful achievement and worth the effort.

Peace is a preliminary step towards experiencing a state of lasting bliss. While attaining peace is no small feat, reaching bliss is even more challenging because the spiritual journey to attain it starts from peace. If we aspire to be peaceful, we can attain peace by developing contentment, managing stress and moderating our tendencies. Unfortunately, by the time we mature enough to seek peace, we have accumulated a great deal of anxiety, stress and loneliness that weigh on our bodies and minds. Therefore, it's best to seek peace when we are young, so we are less weighed down and have more time to attain bliss as we age. However, this does not mean that bliss is unattainable for adults. Not at all.

Many of us, perhaps especially those who come from South Asian families, as I do, were raised with a strong focus on studies and material success. This was particularly true for those without generational wealth to rely on. Although we had some exposure to the concept of peace, mostly during religious festivals, it was largely limited to ritualistic practices, and its deeper meaning was not fully understood or applied.

Personally, I was fortunate to find meditation intriguing and began to develop a thirst for self-realization. However, many of my childhood friends are seeking peace now at an age when it becomes more challenging to establish new habits like meditation. Even though the process of rewiring our brains and sustaining new habits becomes more difficult in later years, the study of neuroplasticity provides hope that we can still make progress, even if we start late.

Bliss and Beyond

Bliss is a more profound and enduring state than peace because it emanates from our inner being. It can be considered a *spiritual condition* that remains unaffected by changing circumstances. Bliss encompasses the strength and awareness to remain steadfast during the ups and downs of life. It is the result of our mastery over the ordinary aspects of existence. Unlike peace, which is defined by serenity and the absence of disturbance, bliss is an active, overwhelming sense of joy that transcends ordinary happiness. It is often associated with moments of spiritual awakening, deep connection or the realization of one's desires. Bliss is typically more fleeting than peace, a momentary glimpse of ultimate contentment that can feel transcendent or otherworldly.

If bliss is a state beyond peace, is there anything beyond bliss? According to my spiritual teacher, the answer is reality itself. In many spiritual traditions, the combination of existence, truth, knowledge, consciousness and bliss is considered the culmination of all spiritual practices in life. In Hindu philosophy, this is known as *sat chit ananda*, signifying the highest state a spiritual seeker can achieve.

This is also considered the state of all-pervasive, ultimate reality or the oneness that represents the omnipresence of God. '*Satyam Jnanam Anantham Brahman*' is a chant recited by many spiritual devotees across India. In English, it means, 'Truth, knowledge and bliss is the ultimate reality or oneness of godliness.'

Bliss is beyond peace and characterized by a profound, stable inner serenity unaffected by external circumstances. The paradoxical twist is that while bliss is depicted as an attainable state, once one becomes blissful, there is no more one; the experience transcends personal experience. The paradox lies in *experiencing* bliss when, by its very nature, becoming truly blissful means transcending the individual capacity to experience anything as the self dissolves into a greater reality.

While seeking bliss implies a quest for something extraordinary, does true contentment (peace) actually require the relinquishing of such pursuits, embracing simplicity and finding joy in the mundane? Does it involve finding a deep, enduring sense of contentment in the acceptance of the present moment? If we find peace in the simplicity and acceptance of everyday live, do we stop seeking bliss and beyond altogether?

Not at all. One way to explain how we would feel and experience bliss, is to know that it is the penultimate human experience before uniting with the ultimate reality or the absolute. Although the practice of Heartfulness meditation can take you on an infinite journey, do not worry about the outcome. It is sufficient for most people to aim for peace when they do their daily practice. Aim for peace and then cultivate it further (by continuing your practice) to bliss and beyond over the course of your lifespan.

What does it feel like to experience absolute bliss? In my book with Joshua Pollock, *The Heartfulness Way*, I explain: 'When I am dissolved in the Ultimate Source, it is absolute bliss. Rather I become bliss. And when I become bliss, how can I experience it? It is like a raindrop that falls into the ocean. There is no more drop. It has become the ocean, you see.'[1]

What happened to the drop? Where did it go? It can't be found as something any more. It became nothing. Or did it? It became a part of everything, which is the same as nothingness! In this coming together of nothingness and 'everythingness' is the complete expansion of our consciousness. When such a consciousness is available to us, we too become the son of the father, the children of God, or Buddha-like, Christ-like, or we attain Krishna Consciousness or Christ consciousness. We go from peace to bliss and to beyond!

Part 6

Toolbox: Suggested Practices and Exercises

Exercises

In this section, I suggest a few exercises and affirmations for daily reflection, to reset your thoughts and actions. These are tools you can use every day. Taking the time to reflect is critical in stress management and self-realization. At first glance, these exercises may appear similar. But as you practise them and experience the benefit of each one, you will develop a better appreciation for the subtle differences.

For all exercises (except Relax and Rejuvenate) you'll identify your intention, your reason for doing the exercise and an action you might take towards that intention. In the Pause exercise, you'll find an example of how you might phrase these three items. Consider writing these down before the exercise. You might change them each time you do the exercise or keep them as they are until you feel inclined to change them. You can enter new versions in your paper or digital notebook. If you prefer, you can first meditate to discover your intention, reason and action, and then do the exercise.

Entering the intention, reason and action for each exercise helps you become much more engaged in the exercise and derive so much more from it. I suggest recording the exercise in your own voice or have someone you love and trust record the exercise for you. That way, when you're ready, you can just close your eyes and begin. After you've completed the exercise, you can enter your thoughts in your notebook.

When you first begin practising these exercises, follow the order they're listed in because each one builds on skills mastered in the preceding exercise. After that, you can get creative. These exercises are suggestions; experiment with them. Mix and match. As you practise, you'll become increasingly knowledgeable about which tool to use when and what modifications might help most. Have fun!

Notes:

- In a few select chapters, I offer questions or invite you to reflect. You may apply these types of introspective questions to other chapters as well. The meditation exercises in this section provide a framework for reflection.
- You can find similar exercises in the Heartfulness App and on the website (See Resources).

For all exercises, you'll begin with the preparatory steps (1–7).

Preparatory Steps

1. Choose a favourite place in your home, backyard or a nearby park to practise.
2. Wear comfortable clothes, including socks or shoes if needed.
3. Plan to avoid all distractions and turn off all notifications on your phone.
4. Keep a digital or paper journal handy to record your thoughts after the exercise.
5. Sit alone, quietly and comfortably.
6. Gently close your eyes.
7. Take a deep breath and let go.

For all exercises, except Relax and Clean, you will continue with the following steps:

8. Focus on your heart.
9. Develop a feeling of love and connection to yourself.
10. Maintain a non-judgemental attitude.
11. Start with naming the **intention** to change the situation or improve your understanding of the situation.
12. Recite the **reasons** to back the intention.
13. Name an **action**—an attitude, an inner condition or a feeling—to support the intention and reason.
14. Do the chosen exercise for about ten minutes, keeping your focus on the heart.

15. If the mind wanders, ignore it and gently come back to the heart.
16. End the exercise with the conviction that the desired positive outcome will manifest in due course.
17. Keep your eyes closed for a few minutes and gently open them with love and gratitude pervading throughout.

Pause

Pausing is not only an exercise; it can also become a habit. In a challenging situation, we must learn to pause deliberately because when we react immediately, without coming from the heart, the tension can increase and the outcome is far from what's best for all.

During the situation, if you notice you're feeling agitated, anxious or angry, pause for a few seconds. If you recognize that you experience these feelings often, make it a point to consciously practise pausing several times a day. If you're busy during the day and can't take short breaks, make sure to practise in the morning and evening. Notice how you feel as you pause, and afterwards. Before long, you'll find that you automatically pause before responding, and the pause may be very brief. Once you master this tool, your pausing becomes more automatic, you can move on to practising more powerful tools.

Intention: I'm developing the ability to pause and be fully present.

Reason: Pausing will help me see things more clearly. It will take me time to understand. I will be able to centre myself and respond to any situation properly to improve the result and reduce the risks of a bad outcome. (You may also think of a situation that has warranted you to practise this exercise).

Action: Try recording the pausing exercise in your own voice or in the voice of someone you trust. Follow the seventeen preparatory steps, adding your intention and reason. Then play the recording and follow your own guided practice. After the recording ends, sit quietly for as long as you like.

Relax

The PEMS model of total health and well-being includes four categories: physical, emotional, mental and spiritual. Physical health also has four pillars, which we refer to as REMS: relax, eat well, move often and sleep. From these models, you can see that physical health is extremely important and relaxing is a critical first step.

Ideally, we practise relaxation daily for 10–15 minutes. This exercise is a progressive muscle relaxation ultimately relaxing the entire body and mind. While I recommend Heartfulness techniques, you can follow any of the videos that are available in apps or online.

The following instructions will guide you through the Relaxation exercise. You may record this script or create and record your own.

Imagine that the relaxing energy from the earth is entering your body through your toes, feet and ankles.

Pause and feel the relaxation for a minute.

Proceed to allow the energy to move up through the calf muscle to your knees, relaxing them.

Pause and feel.

This way you allow the relaxing energy to move up to your thighs and abdomen.

Then to your back.

Then to your stomach and chest areas.

Then to your shoulders, forearms, elbows and all the way to the fingers.

Then the neck.

Then to your face. When you are here, imagine your jaw, mouth, lips, nose, eyes, eyebrows, eyelids, cheeks, earlobes and forehead are all relaxing.

Pause for a minute or longer on each segment so the relaxation is complete progressively.

Now, imagine that the relaxing energy is entering the top, side and back of your head relaxing it and the brain.

Then, scan your entire body from the top of your head to your toes. If you feel any part of the body is not quite relaxed, just imagine more energy flowing to those areas to relax them.

As they do their work, you will feel totally relaxed and calm.

Now, you take your attention to the heart again and finish with a positive regenerative feeling such as love, kindness and gratitude.

Introspect

This exercise is extremely helpful when an action or a situation you encounter during the day simmers and continues to bother you.

To introspect means to see within. To see anything clearly, we need to be free of any mental fog we may have. Before you begin, you might want to do the Pause and Relax exercises so you're calm and clear. During introspection, we can visualize an interaction or situation without any emotional entanglement. This will offer us clarity and we will be able to accept our role in that situation. In addition to this clarity, we may also reflect on what we could have done to improve the outcome.

Refer to the intention, reason and action in the Pause exercise to craft your intention for doing this exercise.

Intention: _____

Reason: _____

_____

Action: _____

_____

_____

_____

_____

_____

_____

Contemplate

To contemplate is to think about or meditate on a situation, idea or anything you need to look at more closely. We contemplate calmly with a mind that is relaxed, fresh and clear. This exercise is best done after learning pausing, relaxing and introspection. Once you reach a level of expertise in these tools, you may go straight into contemplation. Unlike meditation, contemplation can also be done while walking the dog, sitting on a park bench, watching stars and strolling along the beach.

Contemplation is not brooding but having the situation in mind and keeping an open mind for answers to be revealed from within. The power of the mind will display itself for your self-discovery. This exciting process will inspire you further.

Irrespective of how you choose to contemplate, you could either write the following down or make a mental note as you start your contemplative exercise.

Intention: _____

Reason: _____

_____

Action: _____

_____

_____

_____

_____

_____

_____

Visualize

As with introspection, this exercise can be extremely helpful when an action or a situation you encountered during the day simmers and continues to bother you. This exercise is beneficial when you want to recall and reset repeated behaviours or patterns to create a positive environment for a new outcome in the future. By doing so, you'll diminish the negative emotions you associate with people who have left a bad impression in the past.

1. Begin with the seven preparatory steps of relaxing and sitting down with eyes closed and breathing normally.
2. Recall the situation you were in that requires change.
3. Visualize the situation without any emotion since you are in a safe place now.
4. Recall the specifics of that situation, including what you were wearing, the smell of the room, facial expressions and so on—all while maintaining a non-judgemental attitude.
5. Recall the interaction and, if you can, figure out where things began to veer out of control or led to an unpleasant zone.

6. Now, visualize seeing and talking to that person comfortably throughout the remainder of the exercise.

7. Also visualize a better outcome and the specific steps you would take to create that outcome.

8. If you have made a mistake or if the other person is angry, then visualize love emanating from your heart, its vibrations reaching the other person. Feel the emotions of gratitude, forgiveness or compassion as needed.

9. Do the exercise for about ten minutes, keeping your focus on your heart.

10. End the exercise with the conviction that the desired positive outcome will manifest in due course.

In real life, we may not be able to predict exactly how an interaction will go the next time we're in a similar situation with the same people, but chances are, it will be much better. After completing this exercise, remain alert to future interactions, and open to pivoting the next interaction from a potential negative outcome to a positive one.

Intention: _____

Reason: _____

_____

Action: _____

_____

_____

Meditate

Although the terms meditation, introspection and contemplation are often used interchangeably, it helps to know how they differ. The purpose of meditation is to focus on an idea, returning to that idea when the mind wanders. When we sit in a quiet place with our eyes closed, our senses are muted or drawn inwards. Because of this, our mind tends to wander more when we meditate. When we meditate on a positive, regenerative idea—such as compassion, expansion, forgiveness or love—that idea provides an anchor for the wandering mind to return to and rest on as long as possible. When the mind wanders again, we bring it back to the positive idea. When we meditate in this manner repeatedly, over time, our practice moves up a notch!

Heartfulness meditation is designed to help practitioners regulate, relax the mind and expand consciousness, eventually leading to a permanently awakened state, not only during meditation but at all other times.

Wandering per se is not bad. But if it is a worrying or brooding type of wandering, then it deepens the quagmire we are trying to get out of. So, gentleness and a return to positive, regenerative thoughts are needed. These positive regenerative thoughts are scientifically proven to have a positive effect on our state of mind. They are love, kindness, generosity, compassion, forgiveness, hope, courage, peace and contentment. These words exude certain thoughts, feelings and vibrations which in turn influence our interactions with others.

After the preparatory steps of the meditation, you may choose a specific thought as your anchor thought. For example, 'My heart is filled with love' might be your anchor thought. Those practising HeartMath might keep one of the positive, regenerative thoughts in mind while breathing through the heart. In mindfulness practice, meditators are asked to observe the body and surroundings non-judgementally. In other systems, the focus is on the mantra, breath, forehead or a lit candle.

In Heartfulness meditation, we focus on the heart. We are asked to consider the thought that we are connected to a great Source of all, which is love and light, positive and purposeful. The light from the Source illuminates our heart and mind and this attracts our attention inwards. The positive, regeneratve thought is an anchor that we can return to gently, every time we recognize our mind is wandering. We journey through the various thoughts and emotions and continue to balance and align them. Over time, this connection to the Source, moves us from awareness to a state of absorption. This experience grows on us continuously for as long as we practise Heartfulness meditation.

The Heartfulness Institute and other meditation systems also often provide trainers at no cost to guide you along (See About Heartfulness for contact information).

Intention: _____

Reason: _____

_____

Action: _____

_____

_____

_____

_____

_____

Write down your intention, reason and action for this exercise of meditation. Meditation is normally done in the morning, before you start your day. That said, there is no bad time to meditate, and I don't want to deprive you of the joy of discovering what's best for you on your own. If I had to make a recommendation it would be to meditate when you're least likely to be disturbed. Once you make a habit of morning meditation, the orientation of your practice will evolve in intention, reason and action. As you experience new states of being, Heartfulness meditation continually takes you forward.

Clean

We are familiar with physical cleaning—cleaning out our closets, drawers, house, garden or car. We clean to freshen and rejuvenate our environment, order chaos and create space. Everything feels lighter. We feel fresh and rejuvenated. We think more clearly. We feel more spacious and lighter.

While cleaning the environment does affect how we feel internally, we need to actively clean our minds too. When we feel tired and dull, we often look for activities that refresh us. We start with the physical. We might go for a workout, a run, a bike ride or a hike. Or when we come home, we might wash our face or take a shower. At times, we go out with friends to a bar to have a drink and relax after work.

None of these does anything to reset our mind and ensure the day's mental stress and strain are properly sorted out before nightfall. There is a science behind how our reactions throughout the day makes an impression on our mind. Over time, the predispositions we have along with these new impressions create a new composite. To reverse this process and gain more and more clarity, we clean away the day's unwanted impressions every day in the evening.

This cleaning process helps us maintain better health and manage stress.

This cleaning exercise also uses the autogenic feature of mental suggestions having a desired effect on the body and mind, such as progressive muscle relaxation. But it goes a step further, as you will be using your willpower, determination and conviction to get better.

When you do this exercise don't rush through it. Think about each step and pause between steps. Pausing and reflecting is critical for ensuring this exercise is done effectively. Do this exercise daily for about twenty minutes after work or at the end of a busy day.

After the preparatory steps, the instructions are as follows:

> Put a focused thought that all the unwanted impressions, complexities, mental impurities and emotional heaviness that were acquired and triggered during the day's work are all leaving your body–mind complex in the form of smoke or vapour from your back.
>
> Use this anchoring thought to return if the mind wanders.
>
> After ten minutes, imagine that the love and light from the Source is entering your heart from the front.
>
> It then begins refreshing you and energizing you.
>
> When you recognize you feel light, you end your cleaning with the conviction that you are free of all the unwanted complexities, impressions and impurities.

There are other quick cleaning techniques that can be done on the spot as well. Please refer to the Heartfulness channel on YouTube or in *Heartfulness* magazine.

Inner-Connect

Spirituality is the centre of our well-being. The wisdom is in recognizing this magnificent and complex world we live in. Science alone can't explain it all. For many of us, modern religious practices don't satisfy our search for peace, love and happiness. Both science and spirituality are needed for our total well-being and finding meaning in life.

Prayer is also the cornerstone of both religion and spirituality. In spirituality, the practice of prayer is not about expectation or faith. It is about opening oneself to the possibilities of personal growth and transformation with an attitude of hope and acceptance. Why and how we pray makes a huge difference. Prayer also includes invoking a higher principal or entity to address our prayer to. If we have a spiritual teacher, we can address our prayer to that figure.

There was a spiritual master in India in the late nineteenth century. He did not have a god or a guru so he accepted his schoolteacher as his spiritual master. We all need someone who holds a higher stature than ourselves to help us with what we are praying for. The reason we need an external reference that is tangible is so that we can hold that as a commitment device. It serves us well to remain objective in our spiritual activities and to have an external well-wisher with whom we can interact somehow. They can hold a mirror for us to check our progress. We need this for most of our spiritual journey. When we reach the pinnacle of self-mastery, we may not have an external, living higher entity. But until then, we need someone to hold us accountable for our practice and progress. Having an external reference also avoids self-deception.

This prayer may be done for 5 to 10 minutes. Duration depends on your sense of completeness.

Intention: Achieving the highest possible value for human life.

Reason: We can be better than what we are irrespective of where and who we are. We can be better humans, less afflicted by our desires, emotions and prejudices. We can be aspirational instead of ambitious and filled with self-based desire. We can recognize our tendencies and the need to grow.

Action: We sit in a supplicant mood. Remain open to whatever may come from the Source to help us achieve our intention.

Please note that if you join a system of meditation such as Heartfulness, mindfulness, *vipassana kriya* yoga or mantra meditation system, or any other system, there may be prescribed methods of meditation and prayer for you to follow. In that case, it is better to follow their instructions so you can assess the results they promise.

Alternate Versions

When you have practised these exercises, you will have a better understanding of how they work. You may add to your practices and devise your own exercises of forgiveness, generosity, kindness and gratitude based on what you feel about the reflections for the day. You may send positive vibes of love, hope, peace and well-being to your family and friends.

Try all these and keep journalling. You will be amazed at how good you feel about yourself and others.

Affirmations

Positive self-affirmations are like positive self-talk. I've included a sample of Heartfulness affirmations, but I suggest that you write and experiment with your own to see what works best for you. You can say these affirmations out loud or to yourself while walking, riding your bike, driving or even while sleeping. You can also create your own intention, reason and action exercise. As you recite your affirmations or go through the full affirmation exercise, focus on how the words make you feel. How does it feel to be centred, honest and connected with your heart?

Here is a sample of affirmations you might try.

- I am balanced. I am centred. I am relaxed. I am connected within my heart.
- I am genuine in my intentions. I am developing correct thinking, clear understanding and an honest approach to life.
- I am happy, joyful and grateful for all my life experiences.
- I am becoming more empathetic, compassionate and loving.

- I am clear, calm and confident with my words and actions.
- I feel connected in love to everyone and everything around me.

If you combine breathing with affirmations, you can use the following as an example:

- Breathe in that which is good and positive for your self-improvement.
- Breathe out that which is good for others and for the betterment of the global community.
- Breathe in positivity; breathe out optimism.
- Breathe in appreciation; breathe out joy.
- Breathe in compassion; breathe out love.

Notes

Part 1: Personal Growth and Development

Introduction

1   Heraclitus, *Fragments*, trans. Brooks Haxton, fragment 41 (New York: Penguin Classics; Bilingual edition, 2003), pp. 41–42, kindle.

2   Ibid, p. 95.

3   Lao Tzu, 'The Tao Te Ching', trans. Stephen Mitchell (New York: Harper Perennial Modern Classics, reprint edition, 2006), p. 68, kindle.

4   A.C. Bhaktivedanta Swami Prabhupada, 'The Bhagavad-Gita As It Is', chapter 4, verse 38 (Alachua, U.S.A: Bhaktivedanta Book Trust, 2010), p. 386, kindle.

Stability Promotes Change

1   Bhrett McCabe, 'The 3 Drives in Life: Stability', Bhrett McCabe.com, accessed 3 March 2024, https://bhrettmccabe. com/blogs/blog/the-3-drives-in-life-stability.

2   Paul Main, 'Drive Reduction Theory', Structural Learning, 19 July 2023, https://structural-learning.com/post/drive-reduction-theory.

Motivation Versus Inspiration

1   Oxford English Dictionary, s.v. 'inspiration (n.), sense II.3.,' December 2023, https://doi.org/10.1093/OED/5230 430722.

2   Oxford English Dictionary, s.v. 'inspiration (n.), sense II.3.a,' December 2023, https://doi.org/10.1093/OED/5230 430722.

3   Andrew Thompson, 'Ford's Mission Statement & Vision Statement: An Analysis', Panmore Institute, updated 9 November 2023, https://panmore.com/ford-motor-company-vision-statement-mission-statement.

4   Booker T. Washington, *The Story of My Life and Work*, vol. 1, (Champaign, IL: University of Illinois Press, 1900), p. 126.

Duty or Responsibility?

1   Sri Balagangadaranatha Mahaswamiji, 'Seva is the Spiritual Act of Being Selfless', *New Indian Express*, 17 October 2024, https://www.newindianexpress.com/cities/chennai/2014/May/15/seva-is-the-spiritual-practice-of-being-selfless-612841.html.

Discipline Versus Regimentation

1   Kamlesh D. Patel, *The Wisdom Bridge: Nine Principles to a Life that Echoes in the Hearts of Your Loved Ones* (London: Penguin Ebury Press, 2022), Principle 9.

2   'American Academy of Pediatrics Highlights Causes of Injury, Overtraining and Burnout in Youth Sports', American Academy of Pediatrics, 22 January 2024, https://www.aap.org/en/news-room/news-releases/aap/2024/

american-academy-of-pediatrics-highlights-causes-of-injury-overtraining-and-burnout-in-youth-sports/.

3   Maxwell Maltz, *Psycho Cybernetics* (New York: Tarcher Perigree, 2015).

4   Franklin D. Roosevelt, 'Statement on Signing the Securities Bill', The American Presidency Project, 27 May 1933, https://www.presidency.ucsb.edu/documents/statement-signing-the-securities-bill.

The Tolerance Paradox

1   Aly Juma, 'Buddha and the Wisdom of Acceptance, Medium, 8 April 2016, https://alyjuma.medium.com/buddha-and-the-wisdom-of-acceptance-cf04734ebe9#.

2   Gabrielle Garcia, 'Inviting Mara to Tea: A treatise to learning to succumb to what disturbs you, and accepting any situation, as it is', Medium, 22 July 2016, https://medium.com/clear-yo-mind/i-see-you-mara-come-have-tea-8ca863742be3#.

3   'Causes and Effects of Climate Change', United Nations; Climate Action, accessed 2 April 2004, https://www.un.org/en/climatechange/science/causes-effects-climate-change.

4   David E. Bloom and Leo M. Zucker, 'Aging is the Real Population Bomb', *F&D Finance and Development*, June 2023, https://www.imf.org/en/Publications/fandd/issues/Series/Analytical-Series/aging-is-the-real-population-bomb-bloom-zucker.

The Stillness Paradox

1   Chen-Pang Yeang, 'Discordance and Nuisance', *Transforming Noise: A History of Its Science and Technology from Disturbing Sounds to Informational Errors, 1900–1955* (Oxford, 2023;

online ed., Oxford Academic, 23 November 2024, https://doi.org/10.1093/oso/9780198887768.003.0002.

2 'Relaxation Techniques: Try these steps to lower stress', Mayo Clinic, accessed 19 July 2024, https://www.mayoclinic.org/healthy-lifestyle/stress-management/in-depth/relaxation-technique/art-20045368.

3 Kamlesh Patel (Daaji), 'The stillness paradox', Heartfulness, 28 December 2016, https://heartfulness.org/magazine/the-stillness-paradox-2.

4 Antoine Lutz et al., 'Long-term meditators self-induce high-amplitude gamma synchrony during mental practice', *PNAS* (the Proceedings of the National Academy of Sciences), 101, no. 46, 8 November 2004, pp. 16369–73, https://www.pnas.org/doi/10.1073/pnas.0407401101.

5 Christopher Melinosky, 'What to Know About Gamma Brain Waves, WebMD, accessed 19 July 24, https://www.webmd.com/brain/what-to-know-about-gamma-brain-waves.

Part 2: Emotions and Relationships

The Child Is Father of the Man

1 William Wordsworth, 'My Heart Leaps up when I Behold', *Poems,* ed. Edward Dowden (Boston: Ginn & Company, 1897), p. 137.

2 'My Heart Leaps Up', Poem Analysis, Accessed 5 February 2024, https://poemanalysis.com/william-wordsworth/my-heart-leaps-up/.

3 Krishna Gopal Srivastava, *Bhagavad-Gītā and the English Romantic Movement: A Study in Influence* (Bangalore: Macmillan India, 2002).

4 'How Gita Influenced Romantic Poets', *Times of India,* 21 April 2003, https://timesofindia.indiatimes.com/city/

lucknow/how-gita-influenced-romantic-poets/articleshow/
44006300.cms?utm_source=contentofinterest&utm_
medium=text&utm_campaign=cppst&pcode=461.

5   Jeffrey W. Barbeau, *The Cambridge Companion to British Romanticism and Religion (Cambridge Companions to Literature)* (Cambridge: Cambridge University Press; 2021), pp. 105–120.

6   M.A.R. Habib, 'Introduction to Romanticism', *Rutgers*, accessed 3 March 2024, https://habib.camden.rutgers.edu/introductions/romanticism/.

The Passion Paradox

1   Swami Vivekananda, 'Success', *The Complete Works of Swami Vivekananda* (Delhi: Grapevine India, 2023), p. 748, kindle.

2   Vivekananda, 'Work and Unattachment', *The Complete Works*, p. 65.

3   Vincent Van Gogh, ed. Ronald de Leeww, trans. Arnold Pomerans, 'Arles', *The Letters of Vincent Van Gogh*, New Edition (New York: Penguin Books, 2003), loc. 6984, kindle.

4   Dr Martin Luther King, Jr., 'Love Your Enemies', (sermon, Dexter Avenue Baptist Church, Montgomery, Alabama, 17 November 1957), https://kinginstitute.stanford.edu/king-papers/documents/loving-your-enemies-sermon-delivered-detroit-council-churches-noon-lenten.

The Desire Paradox

1   Ram Chandra, *Reality at Dawn,* abridged edition (Kolkata: Spiritual Hierarchy Publication Trust, 2020), p. 30, kindle.

2   Ibid.

3   Arthur Schopenhauer, *The World as Will and Representation*, trans. E.F.J. Payne (New York: Dover Publications, 1958), vol. 2, p. 573.

4   *Bhagavad Gita*, Commentary by Swami Mukundananda, 2.70, https://www.holy-bhagavad-gita.org/chapter/2/verse/70.

5   Adela Rogers St. Johns, *Some Are Born Great* (New York: Signet, 1975).

If Love Is Blind, Why See Hate?

1   Osho, *Finger Pointing to the Moon: Talks on the Adhyatma Upanishad*, first published in Hindi in 1976 as *Adhyatma Upanishad by Osho* (Zurich: OSHO International Foundation, 2016), p. 31.

2   Victor Kannan, 'The role of the intellect', Heartfulness, 15 February 2023, https://heartfulness.org/magazine/the-role-of-the-intellect-2.

3   R.J. Rummel, ed., *Democide: Nazi Genocide and Mass Murder* (New York: Routledge, 2022), chapter 1, http://www.hawaii.edu/powerkills/NAZIS.CHAP1.HTM.

4   'The Death of Adolf Hitler', The National WWII Museum, New Orleans, 30 March 2020, https://www.nationalww2museum.org/death-of-adolf-hitler.

5   'How to Change the World: One Person Can Make a Lasting Impact', Waterford.org, 9 April 2019, https://www.waterford.org/education/how-to-change-the-world/.

The Loneliness Paradox

1   Dr Jayaram Thimmapuram, 'Alone but not Lonely', Heartfulness, 29 September 2020, https://heartfulness.org/magazine/alone-but-not-lonely.

2   Diel L. Surkalim et al., 'The Prevalence of Loneliness across 113 Countries: Systematic Review and Meta-analysis',

BMJ (*British Medical Journal*) 376 (9 February 2022), no. e067068, https://doi.org/10.1136/bmj-2021-067068.

3   'WHO declares loneliness a health threat, and other health stories you need to know this week', Word Economic Forum, 23 November 2023, https://www.weforum.org/agenda/2023/11/who-lonelines-health-priority-weekly-health-roundup.

4   Office of the Surgeon General, 'Our Epidemic of Loneliness and Isolation: The U.S. Surgeon General's Advisory on the Healing Effects of Social Connection and Community', Washington DC: US Department of Health and Human Services, 2023, https://www.hhs.gov/about/news/2023/05/03/new-surgeon-general-advisory-raises-alarm-about-devastating-impact-epidemic-loneliness-isolation-united-states.html.

5   'Fertility rate in each continent and worldwide, from 1950 to 1924', Statistica, https://www.statista.com/statistics/1034075/fertility-rate-world-continents-1950-2020/.

Thinking and Remembering

1   Julie Tseng and Jordan Poppenk, 'Brain meta-state transitions demarcate thoughts across task contexts exposing the mental noise of trait neuroticism', *Nature Communications* 11, no. 3480 (13 July 2020), https://doi.org/10.1038/s41467-020-17255-9.

2   Attributed to Bishop Beckwith, 'A Logical Proposition', *The Sunday Critic (Critic)*, 22 November 1885, page 2, column 5, Logansport, Indiana. (Newspaper Archive)

3   'Surat Name Meaning', Times Now, accessed 17 October 2024, https://www.timesnownews.com/baby-names/meaning-of-surat.

4   Karen Boyes and Graham C. Watts, *Developing Habits of Mind in Elementary Schools: An ASCD Action Tool*, 2009, (Alexandria, Virginia; ASCD, 2009), p. 297. (Newspaper Archive)

Part 3: Life's Meaning and Purpose

Less Is More

1   'Sustainable Lifestyles in Edo and Japanese History', Japan for Sustainability, no. 7, 31 March 2003, https://www.japanfs.org/sp/en/news/archives/news_id027757.html.

2   Hiroko Oe, 'How centuries of self-isolation turned Japan into one of the most sustainable societies on Earth', *The Conversation*, 9 August 2022, https://theconversation.com/how-centuries-of-self-isolation-turned-japan-into-one-of-the-most-sustainable-societies-on-earth-183557.

3   'Sustainable Lifestyles in Edo and Japanese History', *Japan for Sustainability*, https://www.japanfs.org/sp/en/news/archives/news_id027757.html. [Please add date]

4   'Staff, Japan's sustainable society in the Edo period', *Resilience, 5 April 2005*, https://www.resilience.org/stories/2005-04-05/japans-sustainable-society-edo-period-1603-1867/.

5   Stephen Bradley, 'Why Minimalism Is the Most Important Design Style to Master', Web Design, 9 May 2011, https://vanseodesign.com/web-design/why-minimalism/.

6   'About the Minimalists', The Minimalists, accessed 18 February 2024, https://www.theminimalists.com/story/.

The Correspondence Paradox

1   The Three Initiates, *The Kybalion* (Delhi: Grapevine India, 2023), p. 13.

2   'Hermes Trismegistus', University of Edinburgh Archives Online, accessed on 15 October 2014, https://archives. collections.ed.ac.uk/agents/people/15647.

3   Ibid., p. 14.

4   Ibid., p. 57.

5   Hermes Mecurius Trismegistus, trans. Dr John Everard, *The Divine Pymander*, (Dragon Publishing, 2016), The Eleventh Book of the Common Mind to Tat, p. 65, kindle. (First published [London, Robert White, 1650] for Tho. Brewster and Greg. Moule).

6   Richard Maurice Bucke, *Cosmic Consciousness: A Study in the Evolution of the Human Mind*, reprint of 1905 edition, (Mansfield, CT: Martino Publishing, 2010), p. 3.

The Wish Paradox

1   Ram Chandra, *Reality at Dawn* (Kanha Shanti Vanam: Heartfulness, 2019), 'Realisation'.

2   'Difference Between Self Actualization and Self Realization', Difference Between.net, accessed 26 February, http://www. differencebetween.net/science/psychology/difference-between-self-actualization-and-self-realization/.

End or Means?

1   Niccolò Machiavelli, W.K. Marriott trans, *The Prince* (Delhi: Grapevine, 2019), Chapter XVII.

2   Isaac Asimov, *Foundation,* Revised Edition (New York: Bantam Spectra, 2004), p. 143.

3   Ibid.

4   Louis Fischer, *The Life of Mahatma Gandhi* (New York: Harper & Row, 1950), p. 77.

5   'Swami Vivekananda and His 1983 Speech', Art Institute of
     Chicago,   https://www.artic.edu/swami-vivekananda-and-
     his-1893-speech.

More Is Less

1   Kathryn Spink, *Mother Teresa: An Authorized Biography*,
     Revised edition (HarperOne, 2011), p. 21, kindle.
2   Martin Luther King, Jr., 'My Call to the Ministry', Stanford
     University, 7 August 1959, https://kinginstitute.stanford.
     edu/king-papers/documents/my-call-ministry.
3   'Marie Curie', Britannica, accessed 8 November 2021,
     https://www.britannica.com/biography/Marie-Curie/
     Death-of-Pierre-and-second-Nobel-Prize.

Part 4: Wisdom and Philosophical Concepts

Living to Die, Dying to Live

1   Rachel Fintzy Woods, MA, LMFT, '26 Characteristics
     of Truly Happy People', B.C. Construction Industry
     Rehabilitation Plan, accessed 13 March 2024, https://www.
     constructionrehabplan.com/new-blog/26-characteristics-
     of-truly-happy-people.
2   Liz Mineo, 'Good genes are nice, but joy is better', *The
     Harvard Gazette*, 11 April 2017, https://news.harvard.edu/
     gazette/story/2017/04/over-nearly-80-years-harvard-study-
     has-been-showing-how-to-live-a-healthy-and-happy-life./
3   Sri S.A. Sarnadji, ed., Sayings of Babuji, 6 April 1975,
     http://www.babujishriramchandra.fr/pdfs/saying%20%20
     thus%20speak%20by%20sarnad.pdf.
4   Carl Sagan, *Cosmos*, 1st edition (New York: Ballantine,
     2011), p. 405, kindle.

Two Sides of the Same Coin

1   Dwight D. Eisenhower, 'Radio and Television Address
    to the American People on the Situation in the Middle
    East', The American Presidency Project, 20 February 1957,
    accessed 28 June 2023, https://www.presidency.ucsb.edu/
    node/234105.
2   M.K. Gandhi, *Pathway to God*, First edition (Ahmedabad:
    Navajivan Mudranalaya, 1971), chap 5 (1).

Nice People Finish Last

1   Lynn Seiser, *Why do nice people finish last?: 20 reasons why
    being nice isn't always the nicest way to be* (Aiki-Solutions,
    2019).
2   Richard L. Evans, *Richard Evans' Quote Book* (Salt Lake
    City: Publishers Press, 1971), p. 244, column 2.
3   Sandra Keller, Steven Yule, Vivian Zagarese and Sarah
    Henrickson Parker, 'Predictors and triggers of incivility
    within healthcare teams: A systematic review of the
    literature,' *BMJ Open* (7 Jun 2020), https://bmjopen.bmj.
    com/content/bmjopen/10/6/e035471.full.pdf.
4   'Navigating Leadership: Why Being Kind Beats Being
    Nice', Calix, 18 October 2023, https://www.calix.com/
    blog/2023/10/navigating-leadership-why-being-kind-
    beats-being-nice.html#.
5   'kind', OED, https://www.oed.com/search/dictionary/?scope=
    Entries&q=kind.
6   'kind', Cambridge Dictionary, https://dictionary.cambridge.
    org/us/dictionary/english/kind.
7   'nice', Cambridge Dictionary, https://dictionary.cambridge.
    org/us/dictionary/english/nice.
8   'nice', OED, https://www.oed.com/search/dictionary/?scope=
    Entries&q=nice.

No Good Deed Goes Unpunished

1 Walter Map, trans. and ed. M.R. James, *De Nugis Curialium: Courtiers' Trifles* (Oxford: Clarendon Press, 1983).

2 Saint Thomas Aquinas, *The 'Summa Theologica' of Thomas Acquinas: Third Part* (London: R&T Washbourne, Ltd.,1917), p. 222, https://books.google.co.in/books?id= XwFEAQAAMAAJ&q.

3 Clayton R. Critcher and David Dunning, 'No good deed goes unquestioned: Cynical reconstruals maintain belief in the power of self-interest', *Journal of Experimental Social Psychology* 47, no. 6 (2011): 1207–13, https://doi. org/10.1016/j.jesp.2011.05.001.

Ignorance: Bliss or Sin

1 Katherine Chambers, *Augustine on the Nature of Virtue and Sin* (Cambridge: Cambridge University Press, 2024), chapter 9.

2 'Borrowing Experience', John C. Maxwell, 6 October 2011, https://www.johnmaxwell.com/blog/borrowing-experience/.

3 Thomas Gray, *The Poetry of Thomas Gray: 'Poetry is thoughts that breathe, and words that burn'*, (Portable Poetry, 2014), loc. 613, kindle.

The Science of Spirituality

1 John David, 'The Private Life of Rocks', Philosophy Now, 2016, https://philosophynow.org/issues/117/The_Private_ Lives_Of_Rocks.

2 Becka A. Alper, et al., 'Spirituality Among Americans', Pew Research Center, Report, 7 December 2023, chap. 5, https://www.pewresearch.org/religion/2023/12/07/who- are-spiritual-but-not-religious-americans/.

3   Lauren Valentino, 'Spiritual, But Not Religious', Hinduism Today, 1 July 2017, https://www.hinduismtoday.com/magazine/jul-aug-sep-2017/spiritual-but-not-religious/.

4   *Oxford English Dictionary*, s.v. 'dharma (n.), sense 2' July 2023, https://doi.org/10.1093/OED/5017007965.

5   Daniel Goleman and Richard J. Davidson, *Altered Traits: Science Reveals How Meditation Changes Your Mind, Brain, and Body* (New York: Avery, 2017).

6   'Ikigai', Model Thinkers, https://www/https://model thinkers.com/mental-model/ikigai.

Faith: Belief in the Impossible

1   The Bible, Matthew 17:20, New International Version.

2   Ibid., 17:21.

3   CRISPR: Clustered regularly interspaced short palindromic repeats.

4   Martin E.P. Seligman, *Authentic Happiness: Using the New Positive Psychology to Realize Your Potential for Lasting Fulfillment* (New York: Atria, 2002), p. xii.

The God Principle

1   Aesop, 'Aesop's Fables: Hercules and the Wagoner', Original Sources, https://www.originalsources.com/Document.aspx?DocID=H78RNBBA1CHEGTJ.

2   J.A. Cannon, 'A world in upheaval: Sources of enlightenment', Deseret News, 17 May 2009, https://www.deseret.com/2009/5/17/20318208/joe-cannon-a-world-in-upheaval-sources-of-the-enlightenment/.

3   'Einstein Believes in 'Spinoza's God,' *New York Times*, 25 April 1929, p. 30, https://timesmachine.nytimes.com/timesmachine/1929/04/25/95932842.html?pageNumber=30.

4   Matthew Stewart, *The Courtier and the Heretic: Leibniz, Spinoza, and the Fate of God in the Modern World* (New York: W.W. Norton, 2007), 352. ebook.

5   Qur'an, *Ar-Ra'd* 13:11.

6   'Bhagavad-gītā 6.1–4', Prabhupada Vani, 2 September 1966, https://prabhupadavani.org/transcriptions/bhagavad-g%C4%ABt%C4%81-614/

The Nothingness Paradox

1   Kamlesh D. Patel and Joshua Pollock, *The Heartfulness Way: Heart-Based Meditations for Spiritual Transformation* (Oakland: Reveal Press, 2018), p. 20.

Recommended Reading

I highly recommend the following books for an in-depth understanding of Heartfulness.

Designing Destiny: The Heartfulness Way (New Delhi: Juggernaut Publication, 2022).

The Heartfulness Way: Heart–Based Meditations for Spiritual Transformation, with Joshua Pollock (San Francisco: Reveal Press, 1st edition, 2018; repr., New Delhi: Juggernaut Publication, 2022).

Spiritual Anatomy: Meditation, Chakras, and the Journey to the Center (New York: Balance, 2023).

The Wisdom Bridge: Nine Principles to a Life that Echoes in the Hearts of Your Loved Ones (London: Penguin Ebury Press, 2022).

Stories for Children, retold by Daaji (Kamlesh Patel)

Tales from the Puranhas and Itihaas (Mumbai: Red Panda, 2023).

Tales from the Vedas and Upanishads (Mumbai: Red Panda, 2021).

All the best with this wonderful journey.

Kamlesh Pals.

Heartfulness Resources

I, and everyone at the Heartfulness Institute, would be honoured to support you in your journey to elevated consciousness. Whether you're just learning to meditate or you're a seeker looking to deepen your practice, I hope these resources will be useful to you.

Visit us on our website at https://heartfulness.org

Download our app: https://www.heartfulnessapp.org

Follow us on social media: @heartfulness on Facebook, Instagram and Twitter

Connect with a trainer or find a Heartfulness Centre near you at https://heartfulness.my/heartspots

About Heartfulness

Heartfulness offers a simple set of meditative practices and lifestyle changes. It was first developed at the turn of the twentieth century and formalized into teaching through the Shri Ram Chandra Mission in 1945. These practices are a modern form of yoga designed to promote contentment, inner calm, compassion, courage and clarity of thought. The Heartfulness practices are suitable for people over the age of fifteen from all walks of life, cultures, religious beliefs and economic situations. More than 5000 Heartfulness Centres are supported by many thousands of certified volunteer trainers and practitioners in 126 countries.

Learn more at www.heartfulness.org

Scan QR code to access the
Penguin Random House India website